HISTORY NOTES
Mark E. Hellstern
Tulsa Community College

THE AMERICAN JOURNEY
VOLUME 2
FOURTH EDITION

David Goldfield
University of North Carolina–Charlotte

Carl Abbott
Portland State University

Virginia DeJohn Anderson
University of Colorado, Boulder

Jo Ann E. Argersinger

Peter H. Argersinger
Southern Illinois University

William L. Barney
University of North Carolina–Chapel Hill

Robert M. Weir
University of South Carolina

PEARSON

Prentice
Hall

Upper Saddle River, New Jersey 07458

© 2007 by PEARSON EDUCATION, INC.
Upper Saddle River, New Jersey 07458

ISBN 0-13-237077-8

Printed in the United States of America

Table of Contents

Chapter Sixteen
Reconstruction
1865–1877

KEY TOPICS

- **Advocating the "Lost Cause"**
- **Reconstruction's Impact**
- **Reconstruction's Phases**
- **Reconstruction's Legacy**

CHAPTER NOTES

In the space below, create your own outline of the chapter. Consider the Key Topics above as well as the overall thrust of the chapter and the text's presentation of material.

Multiple Choice: In the blanks below, write the letter of the **best** response.

1. _____ Among the problems faced by the South at the end of the Civil War was (were)
   a. long unattended cropland.
   b. destroyed infrastructure.
   c. a worthless currency.
   d. lawlessness.
   e. all of these problems.

2. _____ For most southern whites, their psychological response to defeat was to
   a. deny that military defeat had actually occurred.
   b. place blame for their defeat on their military leaders, especially Robert E. Lee.
   c. acknowledge that slavery had, in fact, been morally indefensible and that their defeat was deserved.
   d. elevate their rebellion to a noble and holy crusade fought by chivalrous and saintly men.
   e. allow (though grudgingly) freed slaves to assume social equality.

3. _____ Following the Civil War, white southerners
   a. wrote their history books to reflect the nobility of the "lost cause."
   b. moved quickly to restore as much of the old order as possible.
   c. resented attempts by northerners to furnish assistance.
   d. pressed firmly to keep freed blacks "in their place."
   e. did all of these things.

4. _____ Following the Civil War, black southerners
   a. framed the war in biblical terms.
   b. wanted land, civil rights, and education — but also to be left alone.
   c. moved to the West and to northern cities.
   d. became tenant sharecroppers, usually on the land of their old masters.
   e. did all of these things.

5. _____ Following the Civil War, northern whites
   a. put the war into history books and moved on.
   b. became preoccupied with their business and industry.
   c. became less and less interested in the plight of the post-war South.
   d. could not figure out who should control the reconstruction process.
   e. did all of these things.

6. _____ Because of segregation, the "training ground" for generations of African American political, economic, and social leadership was often the
   a. years of Radical Republican rule.
   b. Freedmen's Bureau.
   c. public school system.
   d. black churches.
   e. local factory.

7. _____ Lincoln's lenient policy regarding reconstruction was called the
   a. Ten Percent Plan.
   b. Freedmen's Bureau.
   c. Wade Davis Plan.
   d. Southern Homestead Act.
   e. Half-way Covenant.

8. _____ Andrew Johnson's troubles as president arose from his
   a. lack of political savvy, his inflexible temperament, and his belligerence.
   b. seeming vacillation between parties and viewpoints.
   c. continuous vetoes of important Republican reconstruction bills.
   d. profuse pardoning of former Confederate officials.
   e. all of these factors.

9. _____ Which post-war amendment gave black males the right to vote?
   a. Thirteenth
   b. Fourteenth
   c. Fifteenth
   d. all of these amendments

10. _____ When Congress took over the Reconstruction process, they
    a. created military districts in the South.
    b. disenfranchised many white southerners who had supported the Confederacy.
    c. made it more difficult for states to be re-admitted to the Union.
    d. secured freedmen's right to vote.
    e. accomplished all of these.

11. _____ Andrew Johnson was
    a. impeached by the House of Representatives but acquitted by the Senate.
    b. neither impeached by the House of Representatives nor acquitted by the Senate.
    c. impeached by the House of Representatives, convicted by the Senate, and removed from office.
    d. re-elected in 1868 for a full term of his own.

12. _____ The term "bloody shirt" referred to
    a. a cherished heirloom owned by the widow of Abraham Lincoln.
    b. a Civil War-era relic on display at the Smithsonian Institute.
    c. a campaign technique employed by post-war Republicans to remind voters of the Democrats' "treason" during the Civil War era.
    d. a secret identifying signal employed by members of the Ku Klux Klan.

13. _____ Native white southerners who defied neighbors and joined the Republican ranks were called
    a. carpetbaggers.
    b. renegades.
    c. redeemers.
    d. things that cannot be repeated.
    e. scalawags.

14. _____ Most of the "carpetbaggers" who arrived in the South wanted to line their pockets at southerners' expense.
    a. True
    b. False

15. _____ There were no African American members of Congress until the 1930s.
    a. True
    b. False

16. _____ Republicans in the South fell into disharmony and out of power because of
    a.   the liberal use of political patronage.
    b.   high state tax rates to fund their activist agendas.
    c.   class and racial tensions.
    d.   all of these situations.

17. _____ The initial (though short-lived) purpose of the Ku Klux Klan was to be a
    a.   forum for political discussion.
    b.   social club.
    c.   Democratic "think tank."
    d.   terrorist group advocating white supremacy.

18. _____ By 1870, "liberal" Republicans were advocating all of the following **except**
    a.   civil service reform.
    b.   higher tariff rates to promote southern industry.
    c.   an end to federal land grants for railroads.
    d.   a general amnesty for white people.

19. _____ Nationally, Democratic Party hopes for victory in the 1876 presidential election
    were raised because
    a.   of Grant administration scandals.
    b.   northern exasperation with southern Republican governments.
    c.   economic depression.
    d.   of all of these factors.

20. _____ The presidential election of 1876 was decided by
    a.   the popular vote.
    b.   the electoral vote.
    c.   the House of Representatives.
    d.   a coin toss.
    e.   a specially created commission.

21. _____ For generations, white southerners employed the "memory of reconstruction" to
    a.   mean "redemption" from black rule and federal oppression.
    b.   underscore the period, as they did the war itself, as a glorious crusade.
    c.   turn textbooks and movies into propaganda.
    d.   nurture racism in generations of southerners.
    e.   accomplish all of these.

Chronological Arrangement: Re-arrange the list of events below by re-writing each item in correct chronological sequence into the blanks provided.

Ku Klux Klan founded   _____

Compromise of 1877   _____

Panic of 1873   _____

Ulysses Grant first elected president   _____

Tenure of Office Act passed   _____

Lincoln proposes the Ten Percent Plan   _____

House impeaches Andrew Johnson   _____

Hayes/Tilden outcome contested   _____

Fifteenth Amendment ratified   _____

Andrew Johnson becomes president   _____

Essay: Read each of the following questions, take some time to organize your thoughts, then compose thorough, meaningful answers for each.

1. List and discuss the major problems faced by the United States at the end of the Civil War.

2. In what ways did post-war African Americans adjust to their new freedom?

3. How did Andrew Johnson's background and life experiences contribute to his version of Reconstruction?

4. Describe the struggle that developed between President Johnson and Congress over Reconstruction. How was the problem "resolved"?

5. How did blacks achieve — and then lose — political power in the South following the war?

6. Discuss the rise of white supremacist groups such as the Ku Klux Klan.

7. Why did the North eventually turn its back on the South?

8. How did the presidential election of 1876 relate to the end of Reconstruction?

9. Why could it be said that the South "won" the Civil War?

10. In your opinion, what could have been done differently to make Reconstruction a success?

Matching: Match each description in the left column with the Reconstruction-era political party most likely to reflect it.

1. _____ Most southern white voters

2. _____ Most southern black voters

3. _____ Carpetbaggers

4. _____ Klan members

5. _____ Used religious metaphors to explain their position

6. _____ Manipulated memories of Reconstruction to maintain power

7. _____ Scalawags

8. _____ Created southern solidarity by race-baiting and violence

9. _____ Benefited from the post-war economic boom

10. _____ Southern black legislators

11. _____ Waved the "bloody shirt"

12. _____ Claimed presidential victory in 1876

A. Democratic

B. Republican

C. Both Parties

Matching: Match each description in the left column with the person it most likely describes. (Beware: Not all names will be used!)

1. _____ The "patron saint" of the "lost cause;" a symbol of piety and poignant nobility.

2. _____ His "Field Order No. 15" fueled rumors that blacks would be receiving "forty acres and a mule."

3. _____ Returned confiscated land to Confederates; vetoed reconstruction measures; opposed Fourteenth Amendment.

4. _____ Lincoln's — then Johnson's — Secretary of War; his firing led to Johnson's impeachment.

5. _____ Suffragist who opposed the Fifteenth Amendment because it extended the vote only to males.

6. _____ Former Confederate cavalry general; his "social club" turned racist and violent almost immediately.

7. _____ Turned Democratic Tammany Hall into a machine that robbed New York of $100 million.

8. _____ Northern general; though elected president twice, his two terms were tarnished by scandals.

9. _____ Reviled Southern general; became the Republican Chief of Police in New Orleans.

10. _____ Won both the popular and electoral votes in 1876, yet did not get to deliver his inaugural speech.

11. _____ Was declared the winner in 1876 — in exchange for the end of Reconstruction in the South.

12. _____ Though he freed his nation's serfs, he did not free them from a plight similar to African Americans'.

A. Alexander II

B. Susan B. Anthony

C. George A. Custer

D. William ("Boss") Tweed

E. Robert E. Lee

F. Nathan B. Forrest

G. Ulysses Grant

H. Rutherford B. Hayes

I. Ivan the Terrible

J. Andrew Johnson

K. Kirby Smith

L. James Longstreet

M. Edwin M. Stanton

N. Nicholas II

O. Oliver Howard

P. Peter the Great

Q. Victoria

R. Edmond Ruffin

S. Samuel J. Tilden

T. William T. Sherman

MULTIPLE CHOICE ANSWERS:

1. E (p. 483)
2. D (p. 484)
3. E (pp. 484–485)
4. E (pp. 484–489)
5. E (pp. 484–485, 491, 499–500)
6. D (p. 489)
7. A (p. 491)
8. E (pp. 492–493, 495–496)
9. C (p. 496)
10. E (p. 495)

11. A (pp. 495–496)
12. C (p. 496)
13. E (p. 497)
14. B (p. 498)
15. B (p. 498)
16. D (p. 499)
17. B (p. 500)
18. B (p. 502)
19. D (p. 503)
20. E (p. 503)

21. E (p. 504)

CHRONOLOGICAL ARRANGEMENT ANSWERS:

Lincoln proposes the Ten Percent Plan, Andrew Johnson becomes president, Ku Klux Klan founded, Tenure of Office Act passed, House impeaches Andrew Johnson, Ulysses Grant first elected president, Fifteenth Amendment ratified, Panic of 1873, Hayes/Tilden outcome contested, Compromise of 1877

MATCHING ANSWERS:

1. A
2. B
3. B
4. A
5. A
6. A
7. B
8. A
9. B
10. B
11. B
12. C

MATCHING ANSWERS:

1. E
2. T
3. J
4. M
5. B
6. F
7. D
8. G
9. L
10. S
11. H
12. A

Chapter Seventeen
A New South:
Economic Progress and Social Tradition
1877–1900

KEY TOPICS

- **Changes in the Post-war South**
- **The Rise of Populism**
- **Deteriorating Race Relations**

CHAPTER NOTES

In the space below, create your own outline of the chapter. Consider the Key Topics above as well as the overall thrust of the chapter and the text's presentation of material.

Multiple Choice: In the blanks below, write the letter of the **best** response.

1. _____ The "New South" was new, mostly in
   a. race relations.
   b. economics.
   c. technological modernization.
   d. education opportunities.
   e. all of these areas.

2. _____ The political party that created a "Solid South" by purging blacks from voting booths and positions of leadership for many decades was the
   a. Democratic.
   b. Republican.
   c. Populist.

3. _____ In the decades following the Civil War, black southerners sought
   a. dignity and self-respect.
   b. employment opportunities.
   c. opportunities to vote.
   d. education and travel opportunities.
   e. all of these things.

4. _____ The economy of the New South witnessed impressive growth and performance in
   a. iron and steel production.
   b. textile manufacturing.
   c. tobacco and lumber production.
   d. furniture manufacturing.
   e. all of these areas.

5. _____ Which of the following southern cities did **not** experience a rise to prominence due to post-Civil War railroad construction?
   a. Dallas, Texas
   b. Atlanta, Georgia
   c. New Orleans, Louisiana
   d. Nashville, Tennessee
   e. Charlotte, North Carolina

6. _____ Southern urban and industrial growth greatly exceeded that of the North in the decades after the Civil War.
   a. True
   b. False

7. _____ Between 1860 and 1900, the *per capita* income of the South actually declined in relation to the national average.
   a. True.
   b. False.

8. _____ Low wages in the South led to all of the following **except**
   a. low consumer demand.
   b. low tax revenues available for things like public education.
   c. the reliance of southern industry on technology and machinery.
   d. the flight of highly skilled and better-educated workers to northern cities.
   e. the choice of immigrants to seek higher wages in the North.

9. _____ By 1900, most small southern towns looked almost the same as they had in 1865.
   a. True
   b. False

10. _____ By 1900, most southern cotton producers
    a. relied on fertilizers to revive nutrient-depleted land.
    b. opened new areas for increased production.
    c. produced more cotton — but made less money.
    d. imported most of their food-stuffs from the North and the West.
    e. did all of these.

11. _____ Why didn't the South seek to limit cotton production?
    a. In their credit-reliant economy, cotton was more readily used as collateral.
    b. Other crops generated less income per acre.
    c. Cotton demand — and therefore prices — abroad remained high.
    d. All of these are correct.
    e. Only a and b are correct.

12. _____ Which of the following is NOT true of the Southern Farmers' Alliance?
    a. It offered members discounts on supplies and credit.
    b. Members collectively marketed their cotton crops.
    c. It linked membership with conservative Christianity.
    d. Membership generally remained small and confined to rural Texas.
    e. It became a surrogate government and church for many rural southerners.

13. _____ Most Holiness and Church of God congregations strictly limited participation by women and blacks.
    a. True
    b. False

14. _____ The innovative "subtreasury" plan
    a. urged cotton producers to store their crops and wait for the best times to sell.
    b. was designed to free producers from merchants' high interest rates and crop liens.
    c. was endorsed by Democratic candidates who then failed to enact it.
    d. led to the demise of the Southern Farmers' Alliance.
    e. involved all of these.

15. _____ The Populist Party began in
    a. Texas.
    b. Wisconsin.
    c. Kansas.
    d. Nebraska.
    e. Illinois.

16. _____ By 1900, most southern blacks were loyal to what political party?
    a. Republican
    b. Democratic
    c. Populist
    d. Progressive

17. _____ As part of their response to Civil War military defeat, southern men
    a. recast the war in terms of a noble crusade.
    b. imagined southern women as paragons of purity who needed to be defended.
    c. cast blacks — rather than the hated Yankees — in the role of the enemy.
    d. did all of these things.

18. ____ White southern men allowed women to participate in church, missionary, and reform groups primarily because
    a. these were deemed to be natural extensions of the home and family.
    b. they realized the moral importance of such efforts.
    c. such involvement would deter them from seeking suffrage.
    d. such efforts contributed to racial segregation.

19. ____ In the decades following the Civil War, which activity generally was kept the most segregated racially?
    a. day-to-day business and commerce
    b. labor in the workplace
    c. church attendance
    d. hunting and fishing
    e. neighborhood housing

20. ____ In the South, it was commonly understood that black men were **not** supposed to
    a. prosper financially.
    b. challenge white authority.
    c. make any remotely sexual gesture toward white women.
    d. try to get out of "their place."
    e. do any of these things.

21. ____ White southern men who lynched black victims did so mostly to restore their own sense of manhood and honor.
    a. True
    b. False

22. ____ Segregation became the official law of the land following the Supreme Court's ruling in the case of
    a. *Worcester v. Georgia*.
    b. *Fletcher v. Peck*.
    c. *Plessy v. Ferguson*.
    d. *Brown v. Board of Education*.
    e. *Miranda v. Arizona*.

23. ____ To circumvent the Fifteenth Amendment and keep blacks from voting, southerners
    a. imposed poll taxes.
    b. established literacy and educational tests.
    c. enacted "grandfather clauses."
    d. did all of these.

24. ____ The white South was able to succeed in instituting white supremacy because
    a. northerners began to agree with southern notions of biological inferiority.
    b. northerners grew preoccupied with matters of business, industry, and foreign affairs.
    c. Republican politicians could count on enough votes from the North and West that they could afford to let the South be Democratic.
    d. of all of these factors.

25. ____ The most successful response(s) to segregation was (were) for southern blacks to
    a. migrate in large numbers to northern cities.
    b. move in large numbers to Liberia in Africa.
    c. withdraw into a rich community life, free from contact and harassment by whites.
    d. remain docile and accept racial roles and stereotypes.
    e. do all of these things.

Essay: Read each of the following questions, take some time to organize your thoughts, then compose thorough, meaningful answers for each.

1. In what areas did the South experience progress after the Civil War? What were the limits of this progress?

2. For many decades — well into the mid-twentieth century — the South was called the "Solid South." What was meant by this? Why did this situation exist?

3. List and describe the major cornerstones of southern economics in the late nineteenth century.

4. Discuss the patterns of urbanization in the post-Civil War South.

5. Discuss the factors that kept the South poor, even during an era of industrialization and urbanization.

6. Describe the economic forces that made rural southerners feel the need to organize.

7. Describe the appeal of the Southern Farmers' Alliance.

8. Discuss the three-party political situation in the South in the last decades of the nineteenth century.

9. List and discuss the various roles played by women in the South.

10. Discuss the "white backlash" against race progress. Why did the North seemingly "approve"?

11. What was the response of the black community and black leadership?

Matching: Match each description in the left column with the person it most likely describes. (Beware: Not all names will be used!)

1. _____ Born a slave in North Carolina in 1858, she earned a doctoral degree at the Sorbonne.

2. _____ Atlanta pharmacist whose headache concoction is now a product consumed world-wide.

3. _____ Wisconsin native; directed the Southern Farmers' Alliance; proposed a subtreasury for cotton.

4. _____ Former missionary in China; opened a home mission in her native Atlanta in 1883.

5. _____ Atlanta suffragist, WCTU member; pushed for school education, but also for white supremacy.

6. _____ Believed his first class train ticket entitled him to first class seating, that the Constitution is colorblind.

7. _____ Former Kentucky slave holder; the only dissenting vote in *Plessy v. Ferguson*.

8. _____ White minstrel-show performer whose "Jim Crow" epitomized the clownish black stereotype.

9. _____ Movie director whose *Birth of a Nation* reinforced a pro-southern view of the Civil War and aftermath.

10. _____ Harvard professor who perpetuated the "scientific fact" of white superiority and black inferiority.

11. _____ Organized an annual Conference on Negro Problems at Atlanta University.

12. _____ Theorized that blacks should "accommodate" to segregation while proving their worth and ability.

13. _____ First African American to earn a Harvard doctrorate; opposed the "Atlanta Compromise."

14. _____ Former Charleston slave pilot; became a member of the U.S. House of Representatives.

15. _____ German Jew who viewed Europeans' growing anti-Semitism and recommended removal to Palestine.

A. Charles Francis Adams

B. Bernard Baruch

C. Anna J. Cooper

D. W.E.B. DuBois

E. Elizabeth Eckford

F. Rebecca Felton

G. D.W. Griffith

H. John Marshall Harlan

I. Billy Ingram

J. John Pemberton

K. Helmut Kohl

L. Laura Haygood

M. Charles W. Macune

N. Asa Candler

O. Richard Olney

P. Homer Plessy

Q. Victoria

R. Thomas Rice

S. Robert Smalls

T. Theodor Herzl

U. John Updike

V. William K. Vanderbilt

W. Booker T. Washington

MULTIPLE CHOICE ANSWERS:

1. B (p. 515)
2. A (p. 516)
3. E (p. 516)
4. E (p. 516)
5. C (p. 517)
6. B (p. 518)
7. A (p. 519)
8. C (pp. 519–520)
9. B (p. 521)
10. E (p. 522)

11. E (pp. 522–523)
12. D (pp. 523–524)
13. B (p. 524)
14. E (p. 525)
15. C (p. 525)
16. A (p. 525)
17. D (pp. 526, 530)
18. A (p. 526)
19. C (p. 529)
20. E (pp. 530–531)

21. A (p. 531)
22. C (p. 532)
23. D (p. 533)
24. D (p. 536)
25. C (p. 537)

MATCHING ANSWERS:

1. C
2. J
3. M
4. L
5. F
6. P
7. H
8. R
9. G
10. A
11. N
12. W
13. D
14. S
15. T

Chapter Eighteen
Industry, Immigrants, and Cities
1870–1900

KEY TOPICS

- **The Industrial Revolution and Its Implications**
- **Immigration and Reaction**
- **Urbanization and Its Implications**

CHAPTER NOTES

In the space below, create your own outline of the chapter. Consider the Key Topics above as well as the overall thrust of the chapter and the text's presentation of material.

Multiple Choice: In the blanks below, write the letter of the **best** response.

1. _____ By 1900, the United States was producing more than one-third of the world's manufactured goods.
   a. True
   b. False

2. _____ During the Industrial Revolution, which of the following was the least important factor in determining a factory's location?
   a. availability of electricity
   b. nearness to a river to provide water power
   c. accessibility of transportation
   d. concentration of a labor force

3. _____ According to the text, perhaps the most important of Edison's innovations was
   a. the electric light bulb.
   b. the electrical vote recorder.
   c. the phonograph.
   d. a model for corporate-sponsored research and development.

4. _____ According to the text, a corporation is an advantageous form of business organization because
   a. it separates ownership from management.
   b. it can raise operating capital from many diverse sources.
   c. a corporation can outlive its founders, permitting long-term planning.
   d. its officials and shareholders are not personally liable for its debts.
   e. of all of these factors.

5. _____ According to the text, corporations changed the nature of work in America by
   a. replacing well-paid, skilled artisans with unskilled, low-paid workers.
   b. locating their factories in cities, thus stimulating urban growth.
   c. creating abundant jobs, but with low salaries and long hours.
   d. luring workers (and their families) from Europe, Asia, and the American South.
   e. all of these changes.

6. _____ "Vertical Integration" involves all of the following **except**
   a. consolidation of all functions related to a particular industry.
   b. reducing a company's dependence on outside suppliers.
   c. handling every aspect of a commodity, from extracting raw materials to selling the finished product.
   d. buying out independent competitors.
   e. geographical dispersal and corporate bureaucracy.

7. _____ In building Standard Oil, John D. Rockefeller practiced
   a. vertical integration.
   b. horizontal integration.
   c. both of these strategies.
   d. neither of these strategies.

8. _____ Rockefeller's near-monopoly of petroleum was broken by the discovery of rich oil fields in Oklahoma and Texas..
   a. True
   b. False

9. ____ New industries that appeared in America between 1870 and 1900 included all of the following **except**
   a. steel.
   b. food canning.
   c. clothing.
   d. cigarettes.
   e. electrical equipment.

10. ____ Which of these industries was **not** notorious for its job-related injuries?
    a. railroad
    b. steel
    c. meat-packing.
    d. coal mining
    e. teaching

11. ____ Among the jobs usually performed by women in the late nineteenth century was (were)
    a. salesgirls in downtown department stores.
    b. office and clerical positions.
    c. elementary school teaching.
    d. nursing.
    e. all of these jobs.

12. ____ According to the text, the most visible badge of poverty was
    a. the location of one's neighborhood.
    b. a thick, foreign accent.
    c. inadequate housing.
    d. one's occupation.
    e. the presence of disease.

13. ____ The "Gospel of Wealth"
    a. stressed hard work and perseverance as necessary for financial success.
    b. argued that poverty was the result of character flaws.
    c. discouraged intervention on behalf of the poor.
    d. argued that the affluent should funnel surplus wealth back into their communities.
    e. asserted all of these.

14. ____ According to the doctrine of "Social Darwinism"
    a. the human race evolves through competition.
    b. wealth reflects fitness, while poverty shows weakness.
    c. charity for the poor was misguided and wasted.
    d. "scientific racism" was justified.
    e. all of these notions were true.

15. ____ Which of the following was **not** an attempt to organize labor?
    a. the Patrons of Husbandry
    b. the Molly Maguires
    c. the Knights of Labor
    d. the Know-Nothings
    e. the American Federation of Labor

16. ____ In which of the following situations were armed troops used to end strikes?
    a. the "Great Uprising" (Railroad Strike), 1877
    b. the Homestead (steel) Strike, 1892
    c. the Pullman Strike, 1894
    d. all of these situations

17. _____ Before the Civil War, most immigrants to America had come from
    a. northern Europe.
    b. southern and eastern Europe.
    c. Asia.
    d. Mexico.

18. _____ In Russia, violent attacks called pogroms were aimed primarily at
    a. Germans known as "Volga Deutsch."
    b. Poles.
    c. Jews.
    d. Muslims.
    e. Christians.

19. _____ When Japanese immigrants began to arrive in the late 1880s, most found work
    a. in mines.
    b. building railroads.
    c. on California farms.
    d. in steel mills.
    e. playing baseball.

20. _____ About half of all immigrants to the United States between 1880 and WWI returned
    eventually to their country of origin.
    a. True
    b. False

21. _____ Most immigrants lived in homogeneous communities isolated from society.
    a. True
    b. False

22. _____ For most newly arrived immigrants, the focal point of neighborhood life was the
    a. workplace.
    b. church or synagogue.
    c. tavern.
    d. local public school.
    e. barber shop.

23. _____ For most immigrants, the choice of employment opportunities was determined by
    a. their skills.
    b. their contacts.
    c. the local economy.
    d. ethnic stereotypes.
    e. all of these factors.

24. _____ Nativism
    a. though present before the Civil War, reappeared in the decades before 1900.
    b. was based on "scientific" racism.
    c. believed in a hierarchy of races.
    d. was fueled by Social Darwinism.
    e. all of these answers are true.

25. _____ The "Great Migration" involved the movement of
    a. Jews from Russia.
    b. southern blacks to Northeastern and Midwestern cities.
    c. blacks from Africa.
    d. cheap labor from China and Japan.
    e. European settlers onto the Great Plains.

26. ____ City centers became the locations for all of the following **except**
    a. residential neighborhoods.
    b. corporate headquarters.
    c. retail districts.
    d. entertainment districts.

27. ____ In the late 1800s, America's new middle class began to include for the first time
    a. lawyers.
    b. doctors.
    c. salespeople.
    d. merchants.
    e. ministers.

28. ____ By 1900, baseball had become popular among the nation's middle class because
    a. it was played on an expanse of green field in a large city.
    b. having no time limit, it was leisurely.
    c. it had clearly defined rules and organized leagues.
    d. games were played on weekdays, reducing attendance by the working class.
    e. of all of these factors.

29. ____ Generally, working-class Americans frequented all of the following **except**
    a. college football games.
    b. taverns.
    c. amusement parks.
    d. restaurants.

30. ____ In his landmark book, *How the Other Half Lives*, author Jacob Riis called attention to the plight of America's
    a. women.
    b. African Americans.
    c. Jews.
    d. poor.

Chronological Arrangement: Re-arrange the list of events below by re-writing each item in correct chronological sequence into the blanks provided.

Haymarket Square Riot   _____

Pullman Strike fails   _____

Knights of Labor founded   _____

Jane Addams opens Hull House   _____

Rockefeller forms Standard Oil   _____

Riis's *How the Other Half Lives*   _____

Centennial Exposition in Philadelphia   _____

Edison unveils electric light bulb   _____

Assassination of Alexander II   _____

Chinese Exclusion Act passed   _____

Essay: Read each of the following questions, take some time to organize your thoughts, then compose thorough, meaningful answers for each.

1. What was Mark Twain trying to say when he called America's Industrial Revolution the "Gilded Age"?

2. Discuss the contributions — specific and general — of Thomas Edison.

3. List and discuss the ways American business was changed by the corporation.

4. Why did skilled artisans become obsolete during America's Industrial Revolution?

5. What points were made by the notion called the "Gospel of Wealth"?

6. In what ways did Horatio Alger's novels reflect "Social Darwinism"? How did they dissent?

7. Why did the American Federation of Labor succeed whereas previous attempts of labor organization had failed?

8. Describe the immigrant neighborhood in late nineteenth century America.

9. How did post-Civil War Nativism differ from the pre-Civil War version?

10. Describe the relationship between newly arriving immigrants and already-entrenched American racism..

11. Describe suburban life at the end of the nineteenth century.

12. "By 1900, the factory worker and the department store clerk were more representative of the new America than the farmer and small shopkeeper." Why?

Matching: Match each description or characteristic in the left column with the time period it most closely reflected.

1. ____ Factories powered by water

2. ____ Factories powered by electricity

3. ____ Corporations

4. ____ Proprietorships and partnerships

5. ____ Transporting live cattle

6. ____ Refrigerated railroad cars

7. ____ A workforce of skilled artisans

8. ____ Low-paid, unskilled laborers

9. ____ Railroad construction

10. ____ Women working as nurses

11. ____ Man coeducational colleges

12. ____ Immigration largely from Ireland and Germany

13. ____ Immigration from eastern Europe and Asia

14. ____ Rise of organized labor

15. ____ Nativism

16. ____ Racism

17. ____ Middle-class, suburban neighborhoods

18. ____ Land ownership the prime symbol of prestige

19. ____ Consumer goods the prime symbol of prestige

20. ____ Team sports for the masses

A. Before the Industrial Revolution

B. 1870 to 1900

C. Both periods

D. Neither period

Matching: Match each description in the left column with the person it most likely describes. (Beware: Not all names will be used!)

1. _____ His New Jersey laboratory became a model for corporate research and development.

2. _____ Built a railroad car manufacturing plant as well as a model community for workers near Chicago.

3. _____ Practiced horizontal integration by acquiring competitors' oil refineries.

4. _____ Automated cigarette manufacturing and endowed a North Carolina university.

5. _____ Horrified American beef consumers with his exposé of the meat-packing industry.

6. _____ Danish-born author who told of the widening gap between America's rich and poor.

7. _____ Her Chicago Hull House was modeled after settlement houses in England.

8. _____ His theory of natural selection was used to explain and justify wealth — and poverty.

9. _____ His rags-to-riches "dime" novels extolled the virtues of individualism, hard work — and luck.

10. _____ His Knights of Labor welcomed women and blacks; pushed for an 8-hour work day.

11. _____ His A.F. of L. was less inclusive than the Knights; emphasized collective bargaining.

12. _____ Used federal troops to shut down the Pullman strike of 1894.

13. _____ With her sister, she offered suggestions about the design and function of the ideal American home.

14. _____ Opened Steeplechase Park on Coney Island, using a giant wheel designed by Ferris.

15. _____ First to suggest that Maxwell House coffee was "good to the last drop."

A. Jane Addams

B. James B. Duke

C. Grover Cleveland

D. Charles Darwin

E. Thomas Edison

F. Henry Clay Fricke

G. Samuel Gompers

H. Horatio Alger

I. Lee Iacocca

J. Jacob Riis

K. Claude Kitchin

L. Julia Lathrop

M. Andrew Mellon

N. Gerald Nye

O. George W. Tilyou

P. George Pullman

Q. Victoria

R. John D. Rockefeller

S. Harriet Beecher Stowe

T. Theodore Roosevelt

U. Upton Sinclair

V. Terrence V. Powderly

W. Woodrow Wilson

MULTIPLE CHOICE ANSWERS:

1. A (p. 549)	11. E (pp. 556–558)	21. B (p. 565)
2. B (p. 550)	12. C (p. 558)	22. B (p. 565)
3. D (p. 551)	13. E (p. 559)	23. E (p. 567)
4. E (p. 552)	14. E (p. 559)	24. E (p. 568)
5. E (p. 553)	15. D (pp. 560–562)	25. B (pp. 570–571)
6. D (p. 553)	16. D (pp. 561–562)	26. A (p. 573)
7. C (p. 553)	17. A (p. 562)	27. C (p. 574)
8. A (p. 554)	18. C (pp. 562–563)	28. E (p. 577)
9. C (p. 555)	19. C (p. 563)	29. A (pp. 576–577)
10. E (p. 555)	20. A (p. 564)	30. D (p. 566)

CHRONOLOGICAL ARRANGEMENT ANSWERS:

Knights of Labor founded; Rockefeller forms Standard Oil; Centennial Exposition in Philadelphia; Edison unveils electric light bulb; Assassination of Alexander II; Chinese Exclusion Act passed; Haymarket Square Riot; Jane Addams opens Hull House; Riis's *How the Other Half Lives*; Pullman Strike fails

MATCHING ANSWERS:

1. A	1. E
2. B	2. P
3. B	3. R
4. A	4. B
5. A	5. U
6. B	6. J
7. A	7. A
8. B	8. D
9. C	9. H
10. B	10. V
11. D	11. G
12. A	12. C
13. B	13. S
14. B	14. O
15. C	15. T
16. C	
17. B	
18. A	
19. B	
20. B	

Chapter Nineteen
Transforming the West
1865–1890

KEY TOPICS

- **The Problems and Plight of Natives**
- **The Mining, Cattle, and Farming Frontiers**
- **The "Americanizing" of the West**

CHAPTER NOTES

In the space below, create your own outline of the chapter. Consider the Key Topics above as well as the overall thrust of the chapter and the text's presentation of material.

Multiple Choice: In the blanks below, write the letter of the **best** response.

1. _____ At the time of American expansion into the West, native tribes were uniformly primitive in economy, religion, and culture.
   a. True
   b. False

2. _____ Native American culture tended toward all of the following **except**
   a. emphasizing community welfare over individual interest.
   b. living in harmony with nature.
   c. maintaining a strict separation of religion from all other aspects of life.
   d. regarding land "ownership" no differently than air or water.

3. _____ Which of the following events represents a rare retreat on the part of the United States in its dealings with Native people?
   a. the Sand Creek Massacre
   b. the Rock Springs Massacre
   c. the Treaty of Fort Laramie of 1868
   d. the Wounded Knee Massacre
   e. the capture of Geronimo

4. _____ To "Americanize" Native Americans, most reformers sought to
   a. prohibit Native ceremonial dances.
   b. encourage individual land ownership.
   c. expose Natives to education opportunities.
   d. force Native children to look and dress like white children.
   e. all of these answers

5. _____ As a result of the Dawes Act of 1887
   a. former tribal lands were broken up and distributed among individual members.
   b. "surplus" lands were made available to white settlers and businesses.
   c. Native people lost more than half of their remaining lands in about a decade.
   d. all of these answers
   e. only a and b happened

6. _____ According to the text, the story of the American West has been over-romanticized.
   a. True
   b. False

7. _____ Most individuals who went west as prospectors for gold, silver, and the like became either wealthy or at least comfortably well-to-do.
   a. True
   b. False

8. _____ Most of the few women in the rough mining camps of the West found work as
   a. waitresses in restaurants.
   b. prostitutes.
   c. miners themselves.
   d. hotel owners and operators.
   e. real estate agents.

9. _____ In Leadville, Colorado, in 1879, there were more saloons than churches.
   a. True
   b. False

10. _____ Most violence in the West was
   a. collective, and racially motivated.
   b. the result of personal or family feuds.
   c. the result of cattle rustling, bank heists, and train robberies.
   d. characterized by one-on-one, face-to-face gunfights at high noon.
   e. associated with bar-room brawls.

11. _____ The Cattle Frontier emerged in the 1860s because
   a. there was a demand for beef among eastern urban society.
   b. the limitless grasslands of the Plains could produce large numbers of cattle.
   c. an expanding railroad network was available to link supply with demand.
   d. all of these answers
   e. none of these answers

12. _____ Which of the following was **not** a famous and frequently used cattle trail?
   a. Sedalia
   b. Chisholm
   c. Santa Fe
   d. (Great) Western
   e. Goodnight/Loving

13. _____ Lawmen in western "cow-towns" spent most of their time engaged in all of the following **except**
   a. maintaining sidewalks.
   b. collecting fines.
   c. arresting drunks.
   d. gun fighting with desperadoes.
   e. regulating prostitution.

14. _____ By 1890, a greater percentage of people in the West lived in cities than in the East.
   a. True
   b. False

15. _____ The "Open-Range" cattle industry declined by the end of the 1880s because
   a. cattlemen had over-stocked the plains.
   b. cattle had over-grazed the plains.
   c. of drought conditions in the mid-1880s.
   d. of record blizzards in 1886–1887.
   e. all of these answers

16. _____ Cowboys on long cattle drives were all of the following **except**
   a. former Confederate soldiers.
   b. black.
   c. Mexican.
   d. Scandinavian.
   e. seasonal employees.

17. _____ The Homestead Act of 1862
   a. provided 160 acres of free land.
   b. did not apply in many former Spanish areas of the Southwest.
   c. revealed a false eastern assumption about the nature of the western family farm.
   d. did not keep railroads and other large corporations from receiving the best lands.
   e. all of these answers

18. _____ The term "Exodusters" referred to
    a. African Americans who migrated to the West and settled in black communities.
    b. long coats worn by cowboys on trail drives.
    c. those who employed "dry farming" techniques on the plains.
    d. blacks who fled to northern cities after the Civil War.
    e. those who employed waterless gold mining techniques.

19. _____ During the decades before 1900, many Hispanic westerners went from being landowners to seasonal wage laborers.
    a. True
    b. False

20. _____ The most common early building component in much of the plains was
    a. lumber shipped from the East and Northwest.
    b. cow and buffalo "chips."
    c. sod.
    d. bricks made from fired clay.
    e. woven grass.

21. _____ One of the most precious commodities in the West was (and is)
    a. beef.
    b. wind.
    c. wood.
    d. wheat.
    e. water.

22. _____ On the plains, church attendance was strictly denominational.
    a. True
    b. False

23. _____ Unlike miners and cowboys, plains farmers were able to avoid becoming entangled in national and international economics.
    a. True
    b. False

24. _____ In the excerpt of Zitkala-Sa, she reveals her greatest resentment in:
    a. strictly regimented eating.
    b. having to learn English.
    c. having to cut her hair short.
    d. living with other girls.
    e. living off her reservation.

25. _____ According to the text, other nations that had a "western experience" included all of the following **except**
    a. Canada.
    b. Argentina.
    c. Italy.
    d. Australia.

26. _____ Today, Native people experience the nation's
    a. poorest health conditions.
    b. highest infant mortality rates.
    c. lowest life expectancy.
    d. highest suicide rates.
    e. all of these answers

Chronological Arrangement: Re-arrange the list of events below by **re-writing** each item in correct chronological sequence into the blanks provided.

First transcontinental railroad   _____

Congress enacts Homestead Act   _____

Cheyennes massacred at Sand Creek   _____

Gold discovered in Colorado   _____

Battle of Little Big Horn   _____

Dawes Act is passed   _____

Chinese massacred at Rock Springs   _____

California Gold Rush begins   _____

Barbed wire patented   _____

First cattle drives to Abilene, Kansas   _____

Essay: Read each of the following questions, take some time to organize your thoughts, then compose thorough, meaningful answers for each.

1. Compare and contrast the treatments of Native peoples by the United States and Canada.

2. Describe the evolution of United States Indian Policy from *relocation* to *reservation* to *assimilation*.

3. Why did mining in the West change from an individual effort to a corporate enterprise?

4. How did the western cattle industry change from the "long drive" to the "open range"?

5. For decades settlers bypassed the Great Plains on their way farther west. List the factors that caused them to try to stay.

6. Describe life on the Great Plains for farming families.

7. Describe the forces that finally enmeshed plains farmers in the national economic fabric.

8. Describe the plight of the young Lakota girl Zitkala-Sa.

9. In what ways have things improved for Native people in the most recent decades?

Map Identification: Using the blank map below, locate each of the following items.

Sand Creek Massacre	Chisholm Trail	Rock Springs, Wyoming
Battle of Little Big Horn	Goodnight/Loving Trail	Abilene, Kansas
Wounded Knee Massacre	Union/Central Pacific	Bozeman, Montana
Virginia City, Nevada	Northern Pacific	San Antonio, Texas
Leadville, Colorado	Southern Pacific	Promontory Point, Utah
Black Hills	Great Northern	Cheyenne, Wyoming

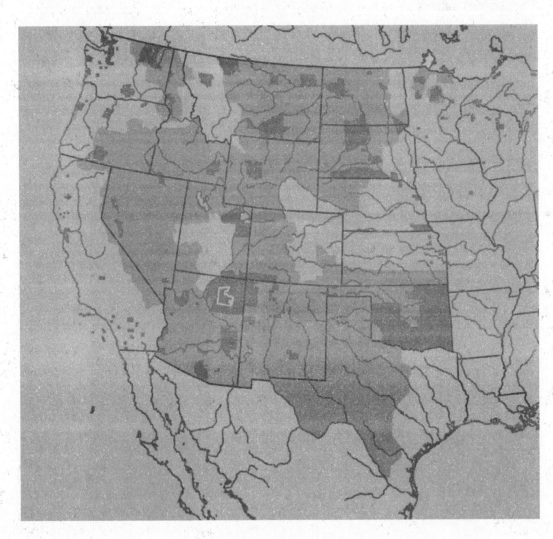

MULTIPLE CHOICE ANSWERS:

1. B (p. 586)
2. C (p. 586)
3. C (p. 589)
4. E (p. 591)
5. D (p. 593)
6. A (p. 593)
7. B (p. 593)
8. B (p. 594)
9. A (p. 595)
10. A (p. 595)

11. D (p. 597)
12. C (p. 594)
13. D (p. 598)
14. A (p. 598)
15. E (p. 599)
16. D (p. 599)
17. E (pp. 601–602)
18. A (pp. 602–603)
19. A (pp. 603–604)
20. C (p. 605)

21. E (p. 608)
22. B (p. 605)
23. B (p. 608)
24. C (p. 592)
25. C (p. 600)
26. E (p. 606)

CHRONOLOGICAL ARRANGEMENT ANSWERS:

California Gold Rush begins; Gold discovered in Colorado; Congress enacts Homestead Act; Cheyennes massacred at Sand Creek; First cattle drives to Abilene, Kansas; First transcontinental railroad; Barbed wire patented; Battle of Little Big Horn; Chinese massacred at Rock Springs; Dawes Act is passed

Chapter Twenty
Politics and Government
1877–1900

KEY TOPICS

- Party Politics, Campaigns, and Elections
- Major Issues: Civil Service, the Tariff, and Monetary Policy
- Problems in the 1890s

CHAPTER NOTES

In the space below, create your own outline of the chapter. Consider the Key Topics above as well as the overall thrust of the chapter and the text's presentation of material.

Multiple Choice: In the blanks below, write the letter of the **best** response.

1. _____ Politics during the late nineteenth century was characterized by
    a. involvement by passionately partisan voters.
    b. record-high voter turnout.
    c. being a popular means of entertainment.
    d. mostly monetary/financial national issues.
    e. all of these answers

2. _____ The positions of the two major political parties on most issues were
    a. boringly similar.
    b. dramatically different.
    c. determined by strong presidential leadership.
    d. driven mostly by social issues.

3. _____ The term "bloody shirt" referred to
    a. a famous Civil War relic on display at the Smithsonian Institute.
    b. a cherished heirloom owned by Mary Todd Lincoln.
    c. a campaign technique employed by Republicans to remind voters of Democrats' treason during the Civil War.
    d. the struggles of sweatshop workers in the garment or "needle" industry.

4. _____ Which of the following groups generally did **not** vote in Gilded Age elections?
    a. African Americans in the North
    b. women
    c. non-citizen immigrants
    d. farmers in Nebraska and Kansas
    e. Catholics of Irish descent

5. _____ Before 1900, elections were usually orderly, well-regulated, and free of corruption.
    a. True
    b. False

6. _____ It was common for major party candidates for president and vice president to be chosen from all of the following states **except**
    a. New York.
    b. New Jersey.
    c. Texas.
    d. Ohio.
    e. Indiana.

7. _____ Which of the following was **not** one of the earliest states to permit women to vote?
    a. Wyoming
    b. Massachusetts
    c. Colorado
    d. Idaho
    e. Utah

8. _____ The Woman's Christian Temperance Union pushed for:
    a. prohibition of alcohol.
    b. strengthened laws against rape.
    c. workplace reform.
    d. women's suffrage.
    e. all of these answers

9. ____ Presidents elected during the last decades of the nineteenth century were all of the following **except**
   a. innovative and dynamic leaders.
   b. conservatives with a narrow view of the presidency.
   c. honest and capable.
   d. forgettable administrators.
   e. detached from concern for social welfare.

10. ____ Though often inefficient, the most important branch of the federal government was the
    a. legislative.
    b. executive.
    c. judicial.

11. ____ Most government employees in the late 1800s were
    a. presidential staff members.
    b. congressional staffers.
    c. postal workers.
    d. law clerks.
    e. unnecessary.

12. ____ In the early Gilded Age, most government positions were awarded on the basis of
    a. seniority.
    b. merit.
    c. party loyalty.
    d. qualifications.
    e. SAT scores.

13. ____ In the late nineteenth century most election outcomes were determined by
    a. candidates' positions on civil service reform.
    b. candidates' positions on the tariff.
    c. candidates' positions on monetary issues.
    d. parties' abilities to mobilize voters.
    e. parties' abilities to "sling mud."

14. ____ Civil service reform became a pressing issue after
    a. the "Crime of 1873."
    b. the disputed election of 1876.
    c. the assassination of James Garfield.
    d. Grover Cleveland's non-consecutive elections.
    e. the rise of the Populists.

15. ____ "Mugwumps" were
    a. reform-minded conservatives.
    b. labor agitators.
    c. illegal immigrants who managed to vote.
    d. staunchly loyal Republicans.
    e. socialist midwesterners.

16. ____ When Democrat Grover Cleveland was finally elected president in 1884, he immediately worked to reduce tariff rates.
    a. True
    b. False

17. ____ By 1890, Congress had successfully checked the power of industrial corporations.
   a. True
   b. False

18. ____ The first federal regulatory agency was the
   a. Food and Drug Administration.
   b. Interstate Commerce Commission.
   c. Securities and Exchange Commission.
   d. Agricultural Adjustment Administration.
   e. Bureau of Alcohol, Tobacco, and Firearms.

19. ____ Immediately after its passage in 1890, the Sherman Anti-trust Act was rendered ineffective because
   a. its wording was too vague.
   b. it was weakened by the courts.
   c. presidents made little effort to enforce it.
   d. most Americans still held a *laissez-faire* mentality.
   e. all of these answers

20. ____ "Sound money" advocates objected to a bi-metallic standard because
   a. silver-based currency was more inflationary.
   b. they wanted to limit the money supply.
   c. booming silver production in the West kept dropping the value of silver.
   d. all of these answers
   e. only a and c.

21. ____ The first group to experience the financial woes that would eventually affect all Americans in the 1890s was
   a. silver miners.
   b. farmers.
   c. southerners.
   d. African Americans.
   e. the steel industry.

22. ____ The "Farmers' Alliance" wanted
   a. regulation of railroads.
   b. federal loans to farmers.
   c. a subtreasury system.
   d. an expanded money supply.
   e. all of these answers

23. ____ The Populist party won all of the following **except**
   a. seats in several state legislatures.
   b. Congressional seats in some states.
   c. governorships in some states.
   d. elections in southwestern territories such as Oklahoma.
   e. the presidency.

24. ____ The "Omaha Platform" called for all of the following **except**
   a. government ownership of railroads, telegraph, and telephone systems.
   b. a government-issued currency.
   c. maintenance of the gold standard.
   d. elections by secret ballot.
   e. the subtreasury system.

25. ____ During his second term, President Cleveland demonstrated remarkable sensitivity to the social and economic concerns of ordinary Americans.
   a. True
   b. False

26. ____ In 1893, the American economy collapsed because of
   a. railroad overexpansion.
   b. a weak banking system.
   c. plunging agricultural prices.
   d. reduced American exports.
   e. all of these answers

27. ____ Grover Cleveland joined Congress in taking decisive measures to respond to the deepening depression of the 1890s.
   a. True
   b. False

28. ____ Jacob Coxey and his followers proposed government public works programs to
   a. be financed with paper money.
   b. create jobs for the unemployed.
   c. improve the nation's infrastructure.
   d. provide an inflationary stimulus to counteract the depression's deflation.
   e. all of these answers

29. ____ In the presidential election of 1896, Democrats relied mostly on
   a. the youth and eloquence of William Jennings Bryan.
   b. a generously funded campaign "war-chest."
   c. the refusal of William McKinley to leave his front porch.
   d. financial support from the eastern business establishment.
   e. their ability to link Bryan with the still-popular Cleveland.

30. ____ By 1900, economic prosperity had returned for all of these reasons **except**
   a. McKinley's record high tariff rates.
   b. revived world markets.
   c. monetary inflation stimulated by gold finds in Alaska, Australia, and South Africa.

Chronological Arrangement: Re-arrange the list of events below by **re-writing** each item in correct chronological sequence into the blanks provided.

James Garfield assassinated   _____

Interstate Commerce Act enacted   _____

Cleveland defeats Harrison   _____

Democrats/Populists choose Bryan   _____

Cleveland defeats Blaine   _____

Silver is demonetized   _____

Panic of 1893   _____

Disputed election of Rutherford B. Hayes _____

202

Harrison defeats Cleveland   _____

Pendleton Civil Service Act passed   _____

Essay: Read each of the following questions, take some time to organize your thoughts, then compose thorough, meaningful answers for each.

1. Why was politics such popular entertainment during the late nineteenth century?

2. Describe balloting procedures in the late nineteenth century.

3. Why was the Civil War still a campaign issue long after the Civil War was over?

4. Who were "Mugwumps," and what function did they serve in the late 1800s?

5. Discuss the rise and influence of the Women's Christian Temperance Union.

6. Discuss the usual late nineteenth century interpretation of the role of President of the United States.

7. How did Lord James Bryce answer the question: "Why great men are not chosen presidents"?

8. How did the federal bureaucracy of the late 1800s differ from that of today?

9. Discuss the positions of the major parties on civil service reform.

10. Discuss the positions of the major parties on tariff rates.

11. Discuss the positions of the major parties on the coinage of silver.

12. Discuss the role of the Populist Party in the "three-way" election of 1896.

Matching: Match each description or characteristic in the left column with the Gilded Age (1870–1900) political party most closely associated with that description.

1. _____ Most African Americans

2. _____ The white South

3. _____ The urban Northeast

4. _____ The northern Plains

5. _____ Farmers

6. _____ Catholics

7. _____ The Midwest

8. _____ Dominated the federal branches of government

9. _____ Recent immigrants

10. _____ Those of German and Scandinavian descent

11. _____ Wanted immigration restriction

12. _____ Avoided confronting the money issue (before 1890)

13. _____ Favored coinage of silver (after 1896)

14. _____ Believed the presidency to be administrative, not creative

15. _____ Favored limited government

16. _____ Favored a federal government actively involved in solving people's problems

17. _____ Favored Chinese exclusion

18. _____ Voted for tariffs that favored their districts

19. _____ Responded quickly to combat the depression of the 1890s

20. _____ Firmly entrenched in the White House for years after 1896

A. Democratic

B. Republican

C. Populist

D. Democratic and Republican

E. Democratic and Populist

F. none of these answers

MULTIPLE CHOICE ANSWERS:

1. E (pp. 616–617)	11. C (p. 624)	21. B (p. 630)
2. A (p. 621)	12. C (p. 625)	22. E (p. 631)
3. C (p. 621)	13. D (p. 625)	23. E (p. 632)
4. B (p. 618)	14. C (p. 626)	24. C (p. 632)
5. B (p. 619)	15. A (p. 622)	25. B (p. 633)
6. C (p. 619)	16. B (p. 627)	26. E (p. 633)
7. B (p. 622)	17. B (p. 628)	27. B (p. 633)
8. E (pp. 622–623)	18. B (p. 629)	28. E (p. 633)
9. A (p. 623)	19. E (p. 629)	29. A (p. 637)
10. A (p. 623)	20. D (p. 630)	30. A (p. 639)

CHRONOLOGICAL ARRANGEMENT ANSWERS:

Silver is demonetized; Disputed election of Rutherford B. Hayes; James Garfield assassinated; Pendleton Civil Service Act passed; Cleveland defeats Blaine; Interstate Commerce Act enacted; Harrison defeats Cleveland; Cleveland defeats Harrison; Panic of 1893; Democrats/Populists choose Bryan

MATCHING ANSWERS:

1. B
2. A
3. D
4. B
5. D
6. A
7. B
8. B
9. A
10. B
11. D
12. F
13. E
14. D
15. A
16. F
17. A
18. D
19. F
20. B

Chapter Twenty-One
The Progressive Era
1900–1917

KEY TOPICS

- **The Origins of the Reform Impulse**
- **Reforming Various Aspects of Society**
- **Reform at All Levels of Government**
- **The Presidencies of Roosevelt, Taft, and Wilson**

CHAPTER NOTES

In the space below, create your own outline of the chapter. Consider the Key Topics above as well as the overall thrust of the chapter and the text's presentation of material.

Multiple Choice: In the blanks below, write the letter of the **best** response.

1. ____ Progressives were unified in their
   a. organization.
   b. leadership.
   c. consensus on objectives.
   d. belief that industrialization had brought problems.
   e. all of these answers

2. ____ Progressivism began when it did in part because
   a. Americans became less complacent and more aware of social and economic inequities.
   b. Americans began to question the assumptions of social Darwinism.
   c. Americans became alarmed when they saw big business become even bigger.
   d. American attitudes were reshaped by liberal clergymen and journalists.
   e. all of these forces

3. ____ In 1911, a fire killed 146 trapped workers at
   a. the U.S. Steel plant in Pennsylvania.
   b. the Triangle Shirtwaist Company in New York.
   c. the Omaha stockyards.
   d. an anthracite coal mine in West Virginia.
   e. the Pullman Company in Chicago.

4. ____ A turn-of-the-century liberal movement in American evangelical religion
   a. questioned the literal accuracy of the Bible.
   b. emphasized the social and ethical implications of the Gospel.
   c. exhibited greater tolerance for other faiths.
   d. resulted in the creation of the ecumenical Federal Council of Churches of Christ.
   e. saw all of these things

5. ____ Journalists who investigated and exposed business and government corruption, dangerous working conditions, and the miseries of slum life were called
   a. yellow journalists.
   b. muckrakers.
   c. socialists.
   d. jerks.
   e. party poopers.

6. ____ Proponents of the "gospel of efficiency" believed that industry should be policed and reformed by
   a. industry.
   b. government.
   c. workers.
   d. city planners.
   e. the military.

7. ____ Members of the Industrial Workers of the World, who employed sit-down strikes, sit-ins, and mass rallies, were known as
   a. mugwumps.
   b. know-nothings.
   c. wobblies.
   d. stalwarts.
   e. party poopers.

8. ____ By 1900, women's roles were beginning to change because
   a. family size was increasing.
   b. women were no longer needed in the workplace.
   c. assumptions were changing about women's natural place as housewives.
   d. labor-saving household equipment required their presence at home.

9. ____ At the turn of the century, most Americans either were **not** aware of or did **not** care about (nor were influenced by) Europe's handling of industrial and urban problems.
   a. True
   b. False

10. ____ The Socialist Party achieved broad popular support at the beginning of the twentieth century.
   a. True.
   b. False.

11. ____ Locally, the Socialist Party won elections in
   a. Wisconsin.
   b. New York.
   c. Oklahoma.
   d. all of these states
   e. none of these states

12. ____ Reacting to the Social Gospel, Protestant traditionalists denounced all of the following **except**
   a. business regulation.
   b. women's rights.
   c. prohibition.
   d. labor unions.

13. ____ The founders of settlement houses reflected the general attitude of progressivism in that they believed
   a. heredity is more important than environment in shaping character.
   b. environment is more important than heredity in shaping character.
   c. society could be reformed by changing individuals.
   d. individuals could be changed by reforming society.
   e. both b and d

14. ____ Between 1890 and 1920, the Supreme Court generally
   a. struck down most progressive legislation.
   b. upheld most progressive legislation.

15. ____ By 1917, most states had some form of
   a. health insurance.
   b. workers' compensation.
   c. unemployment insurance.
   d. old-age pensions.
   e. all of these programs

16. ____ Advances in education by 1920 included all of the following **except**
   a. compulsory school attendance.
   b. kindergartens.
   c. age-graded elementary schools.
   d. pre-school and day-care programs.

17. ____ Most farmers eagerly welcomed educational, societal, and scientific reforms.
    a. True
    b. False

18. ____ The most notable result of the Niagara Movement was the creation of the
    a. NAACP.
    b. NCAA.
    c. FDA.
    d. FTC.
    e. ICC.

19. ____ Which of the following was **not** a democratic reform associated with the
    Progressive Era?
    a. the secret ballot.
    b. direct primaries.
    c. elimination of the electoral college.
    d. the initiative.
    e. the direct election of U.S. senators.

20. ____ (An) advantage(s) of the Australian ballot included
    a. freeing voters from intimidation.
    b. discouraging vote-buying and other corruption.
    c. replacing individual party tickets with standardized, official ballots.
    d. distribution by public (instead of party) officials.
    e. all of these advantages

21. ____ Municipal reforms included
    a. at-large voting.
    b. city commissions.
    c. city managers.
    d. all of these
    e. only b and c

22. ____ Theodore Roosevelt believed that large corporations should be
    a. eliminated entirely.
    b. severely restricted.
    c. broken into smaller components.
    d. orderly and regulated.
    e. left alone to boost the economy.

23. ____ Roosevelt and his successor William H. Taft experienced a falling-out over
    a. Taft's better "trust-busting" record.
    b. Taft's "Dollar Diplomacy" foreign policy.
    c. Taft's firing of Gifford Pinchot.
    d. Taft's background in the judicial branch.

24. ____ Woodrow Wilson's election in 1912 was secured because
    a. William Jennings Bryan opted not to challenge for the Democratic nomination.
    b. Republican voters split between Taft and Roosevelt.
    c. not enough progressive Democrats bolted to vote for Roosevelt.
    d. some more ardent progressives bypassed Roosevelt for the Socialist Debs.
    e. all of these reasons

25. ____ Through two terms in office, Wilson exhibited no flexibility toward progressive aims.
    a, True
    b. False

Chronological Arrangement: Re-arrange the list of events below by re-writing each item in correct chronological sequence into the blanks provided.

Pure Food and Drug Act passed   _____

Ballinger/Pinchot controversy   _____

Women first vote for president   _____

Prohibition begins   _____

Federal Trade Commission created   _____

McClure's begins "muckraking"   _____

16th/17th Amendments ratified   _____

Woodrow Wilson elected   _____

McKinley assassinated   _____

William H. Taft elected   _____

Essay: Read each of the following questions, take some time to organize your thoughts, then compose thorough, meaningful answers for each.

1. Describe some core progressive beliefs regarding the responsibility and role of government.

2. Explain how the "Social Gospel" movement used religious ideas to push for social reform.

3. Explain how social reform often became social control.

4. Discuss the evolution of protective legislation for women and children.

5. Discuss the role played by Margaret Sanger in the evolution of women's rights.

6. What relationship was there between the societal assumptions of progressivism and resulting prohibition?

7. Describe the connection between progressivism and racism.

8. Describe the philosophies that finally achieved a breakthrough to permit woman's suffrage.

9. What philosophy and attitudes of Theodore Roosevelt redefined the presidency?

10. Compare and contrast the progressivism of Roosevelt with that of Woodrow Wilson.

Matching: Match each description or characteristic in the left column with the Congressional Act, Constitutional Amendment, etc., most closely associated with that description.

1. _____ Strengthened the Interstate Commerce Commission

2. _____ Regulated production of foods and medicines

3. _____ Authorized a federal income tax

4. _____ Provided for the direct popular election of U.S. senators

5. _____ Lowered tariff rates, levied first income tax

6. _____ Established a private/government hybrid agency to regulate banking

7. _____ Established an agency to regulate business activity

8. _____ Indirectly prohibited child labor

9. _____ Instituted prohibition of alcohol

10. _____ Established woman's suffrage

11. _____ Allowed secret, orderly voting

12. _____ Allowed citizens to propose legislation

13. _____ Allowed citizens to vote directly on legislation

14. _____ Allowed citizens to vote out an office-holder immediately

A. Australian Ballot

B. Bland-Allison Act

C. Federal Trade Commission Act

D. Dawes Severalty Act

E. Eighteenth Amendment

F. Federal Reserve Act

G. Nineteenth Amendment

H. Hepburn Act

I. Initiative

J. Sherman Anti-Trust Act

K. Keating-Owen Act

L. Smith-Lever Act

M. Recall

N. Newlands Act

O. Harrison Act

P. Pure Food and Drug Act

Q. Indecent Act

R. Referendum

S. Sixteenth Amendment

T. Twentieth Amendment

U. Underwood-Simmons Act

V. Seventeenth Amendment

Matching: Match each description in the left column with the person it most likely describes. (Beware: Not all names will be used!)

1. _____ Explored the social implications of religion by ministering in working-class neighborhoods.

2. _____ Sent his reporters to investigate and expose political and corporate corruption.

3. _____ His *The Jungle* revealed the nauseating conditions in Chicago's meat industry.

4. _____ Imprisoned for his role in the Pullman strike; later a Socialist candidate for president.

5. _____ Baseball player turned spellbinding evangelist, he condemned the social gospel.

6. _____ Believed that schools should be used to promote a progressive agenda.

7. _____ Fled to Europe after she was indicted for distributing information about contraception.

8. _____ Tireless foe of racism; his meeting in Canada led to the founding of the NAACP.

9. _____ Established direct primaries, railroad regulation, and workers' compensation in Wisconsin.

10. _____ Pursued the "strenuous life"; he rejected the custodial role of Gilded Age presidents.

11. _____ Friend of the above, appointed first head of the Forest Service; then fired by Taft.

12. _____ Only president also to be Chief Justice; his politically ineptitude cost him a second term.

13. _____ President of Princeton, governor of New Jersey, gave first State of the Union speech since Adams.

14. _____ Overcame anti-Semitic opposition to become the first Jewish Supreme Court justice.

15. _____ British woman who, with her daughters, fought for woman's suffrage there.

A. Jane Addams

B. Billy Sunday

C. Grover Cleveland

D. W. E. B. Du Bois

E. Emmeline Pankhurst

F. Gifford Pinchot

G. Washington Gladden

H. William H. Taft

I. Louis Brandeis

J. John Dewey

K. Florence Kelley

L. Robert LaFollette

M. Samuel S. McClure

N. Gaylord Nelson

O. Aaron Ogden

P. Mitchell Palmer

Q. Victoria

R. Theodore Roosevelt

S. Margaret Sanger

T. Ida Tarbell

U. Upton Sinclair

V. Eugene V. Debs

W. Woodrow Wilson

MULTIPLE CHOICE ANSWERS:

1. D (p. 645)	11. D (p. 651)	21. D (p. 663)
2. E (pp. 646–647)	12. C (p. 652)	22. D (p. 666)
3. B (p. 647)	13. E (pp. 653–654)	23. C (p. 668)
4. E (p. 648)	14. B (p. 654)	24. E (pp. 668–670)
5. B (p. 649)	15. B (p. 655)	25. B (pp. 672–673)
6. A (p. 649)	16. D (p. 655)	
7. C (p. 650)	17. B (p. 657)	
8. C (p. 650)	18. A (p. 659)	
9. B (p. 651)	19. C (pp. 660, 663)	
10. B (p. 651)	20. E (p. 660)	

CHRONOLOGICAL ARRANGEMENT ANSWERS:

McClure's begins "muckraking", McKinley assassinated, Pure Food and Drug Act passed, William H. Taft elected, Ballinger/Pinchot controversy, Woodrow Wilson elected, 16th/17th Amendments ratified, Federal Trade Commission created, Prohibition begins, Women first vote for president

MATCHING ANSWERS:	**MATCHING ANSWERS:**
1. H	1. G
2. P	2. M
3. S	3. U
4. V	4. V
5. U	5. B
6. F	6. J
7. C	7. S
8. K	8. D
9. E	9. L
10. G	10. R
11. A	11. F
12. I	12. H
13. R	13. W
14. M	14. I
	15. E

Chapter Twenty-Two
Creating an Empire
1865–1917

KEY TOPICS

- Setting the Stage for Imperialism
- The Spanish-American War
- The United States and Asia
- The United States and Latin America

CHAPTER NOTES

In the space below, create your own outline of the chapter. Consider the Key Topics above as well as the overall thrust of the chapter and the text's presentation of material.

Multiple Choice: In the blanks below, write the letter of the **best** response.

1. ____ Most Cubans, Filipinos, Puerto Ricans, and others clearly realized that Americans were motivated solely by their best interests.
   a. True
   b. False

2. ____ The entrance of the United States as a major player on the world's stage was prompted by:
   a. economic self-interest.
   b. social Darwinism.
   c. missionary impulses.
   d. strategic considerations.
   e. all of these.

3. ____ According to a common idea of the time, the "white man's burden" was:
   a. to have to live side-by-side with those of other races.
   b. a duty to aid and uplift people of other races.
   c. to maintain and promote Christianity.
   d. to eliminate people of color.
   e. to take land from people who did not use it efficiently.

4. ____ American missionaries abroad at the turn of the 20th century limited their focus strictly to ministering to the spiritual needs of other nations.
   a. True
   b. False

5. ____ Alfred Thayer Mahan wanted all of the following **except**:
   a. a modernized navy.
   b. a canal to connect Atlantic and Pacific.
   c. naval bases at strategic locations in the Caribbean and Pacific.
   d. for the United States to concentrate on domestic problems and remain isolated from world affairs.
   e. to annex Hawaii.

6. ____ Which of the following was **not** a proponent of "Mahanism"?
   a. Henry Cabot Lodge
   b. Theodore Roosevelt
   c. Mark Twain
   d. John Hay
   e. Elihu Root

7. ____ Most Americans wanted:
   a. expanded foreign markets.
   b. the annexation of as many colonies as possible.
   c. commercial opportunities without actual colonization.
   d. all of these.
   e. only a and c.

8. ____ Many reluctant Americans were persuaded to pursue increased foreign trade by the economic collapse of the 1890s and the resulting unemployment.
   a. True
   b. False

9. _____ According to his letter, Theodore Roosevelt wanted all of the following **except**:
   a. to annex Hawaii.
   b. to build a Nicaraguan canal.
   c. to expel all European presence from the Western Hemisphere.
   d. to aid Cubans in their quest for independence.
   e. to keep from having to use American forces in actual combat.

10. _____ Which of the following colonies is mismatched with the European nation that controlled it in the late 19th century?
   a. Egypt — Britain
   b. Vietnam — France
   c. Congo — Belgium
   d. Tunisia — France
   e. Manchuria — Britain

11. _____ In the 1800s, white Americans began to establish plantations in Hawaii to grow:
   a. pineapples.
   b. rice.
   c. cotton.
   d. sugar.
   e. marijuana.

12. _____ In 1895, the United States intervened in a border dispute between England and Venezuela concerning:
   a. Columbia.
   b. British Guyana.
   c. Brazil.
   d. the Orinoco River.

13. _____ The term "yellow press" referred to newspaper stories that:
   a. hyped stories to attract advertisers, sell more copies, and inflame public opinion.
   b. attempted to suppress Americans' anger and resentment against Spain.
   c. warned of increased immigration from Asia.
   d. warned of the influence of Asian businessmen in American presidential elections.

14. _____ Cuban independence proved to be a major issue in the presidential race in 1896.
   a. True
   b. False

15. _____ In 1898, bowing to intense pressure and fearing imminent war, Spain actually conceded to most American demands.
   a. True
   b. False

16. _____ The _____ was designed to persuade the world that the United States was not intent on annexing Cuba.
   a. Platt Amendment
   b. Nineteenth Amendment
   c. Penn Amendment
   d. Teller Amendment
   e. Gentlemen's Agreement

17. _____ Militarily, the Spanish-American War was conducted with surprising efficiency and skillful management.
   a. True
   b. False

18. _____ Theodore Roosevelt's Volunteer Cavalry in Cuba was known as:
    a. the Texas Light Horse.
    b. the Bully Brigade.
    c. the Rough Riders.
    d. Teddy's Bears.
    e. the Invincibles.

19. _____ Ultimately, maintaining control of the Philippines cost more American lives than had the Spanish-American War.
    a. True
    b. False

20. _____ Which of the following had no "sphere of influence" in China?
    a. Japan
    b. Russia
    c. Britain
    d. France
    e. The United States

21. _____ Theodore Roosevelt's mediation of the Russo-Japanese War culminated in the:
    a. Treaty of Portsmouth.
    b. Open Door Policy.
    c. Gentlemen's Agreement.
    d. Taft-Katsura Agreement.
    e. Root-Takahira Agreement.

22. _____ Which of the following was **not** the location of United States military intervention in the early decades of the 20th century?
    a. Cuba
    b. Guatemala
    c. Haiti
    d. Honduras
    e. Nicaragua

23. _____ In acquiring land for a canal across Panama, Roosevelt did all of the following **except**:
    a. facilitate a Panamanian revolt against Colombia.
    b. act cautiously, trying to bolster American support in the region.
    c. deal with an official of the French Panama Canal Company.
    d. send U.S. naval warships to the region.
    e. violate Colombian sovereignty.

24. _____ William Howard Taft's "Dollar Diplomacy" attempted to control Latin American nations by:
    a. using government action to encourage private American investments.
    b. promoting their internal economic stability.
    c. tying underdeveloped countries to the United States economically.
    d. avoiding blatant use of military force.
    e. all of these measures.

25. _____ Although president Woodrow Wilson apologized to Colombia for U.S. actions regarding Panama, he then became the most interventionist president in history.
    a. True
    b. False

Chronological Arrangement: Rearrange the list of events below by **rewriting** each item in correct chronological sequence into the blanks provided.

Filipino-American War begins   _____

Spanish-American War   _____

Panama Canal opens   _____

Russo-Japanese War   _____

Congress creates Naval Advisory Board _____

Seward buys Alaska from Russia   _____

U.S. acquires Panama Canal Zone   _____

Boxer Rebellion begins   _____

Cubans begin revolt against Spain   _____

Cleveland rejects annexation of Hawaii _____

Essay: Read each of the following questions, take some time to organize your thoughts, then compose thorough, meaningful answers for each.

1. Explain how Leonard Wood's letter reveals essential aspects of America's complex attitudes toward world involvement and influence.

2. How did American racism relate to our expansionist desires?

3. Describe the long and winding road that led to the U.S. annexation of Hawaii.

4. Explain how the "yellow press" played a pivotal role in bringing on the Spanish-American War.

5. Discuss how the question of "manhood"—both generally and specifically—helped to lead the United States into war.

6. Discuss the objections of the Anti-Imperialist League. Why were some more high-minded than others?

7. What were U.S. goals in China, and how were they achieved?

8. Explain the process whereby the United States acquired the Panama Canal Zone.

9. Describe how President Taft tried to soften America's imperialist image.

Matching: Match each description in the left column with the person it most likely describes. (Beware: Not all names will be used. Some may be used more than once!)

1. _____ Philosopher/historian whose speech "Manifest Destiny" preached Anglo-Saxon superiority

2. _____ His book called for a modernized, mechanized, multi-ocean navy, strategic bases, and a canal

3. _____ Wanted to annex Canada and Greenland, but settled for buying Alaska from Russia

4. _____ Native Hawaiian monarch; overthrown by American planters; received President Cleveland's apology

5. _____ His syndicate led by the *New York World* preached that it would be cowardly not to intervene in Cuba

6. _____ Target of a purloined then published Spanish letter, his manhood was questioned regarding Cuba

7. _____ Led a U.S. naval squadron into Manila Bay in the opening action of the Spanish-American War

8. _____ Anti-imperialist labor leader who feared that cheap Asian labor would undercut his workers' wages

9. _____ Feeling betrayed by the U.S., this Filipino guerilla leader had to re-direct his independence fight

10. _____ Ready to seize a Chinese port if necessary, this Sec. of State pushed an Open Door policy

11. _____ Led his own cavalry regiment in Cuba, then helped mediate an end to the Russo-Japanese War

12. _____ Building on the Monroe Doctrine, he recommended the U.S. exercise "police power" in Latin America

13. _____ Proposed using dollars instead of bullets to bind Latin American nations in relaxed ties to the U.S.

14. _____ His self-righteous "missionary diplomacy" led to frequent U.S. intervention in Latin America

15. _____ With Wilson's uncompromising support, this Mexican's revolution toppled his predecessor

A. Emilio Aguinaldo

B. James G. Blaine

C. Venustiano Carranza

D. George Dewey

E. Elihu Root

F. John Fiske

G. Samuel Gompers

H. John Hay

I. Harold Ickes

J. John Jay

K. William McKinley

L. Henry Cabot Lodge

M. Alfred Thayer Mahan

N. Robert McNamara

O. Richard Olney

P. Joseph Pulitzer

Q. Liliuokalani

R. Theodore Roosevelt

S. William H. Seward

T. William H. Taft

U. Victoriano Huerta

V. Pancho Villa

W. Woodrow Wilson

Map Identification: Using the blank map below, locate each of the following places.

Mexico	Cuba	Colombia
Honduras	Haiti	Venezuela
Nicaragua	Dominican Republic	British Guyana
Panama	Puerto Rico	

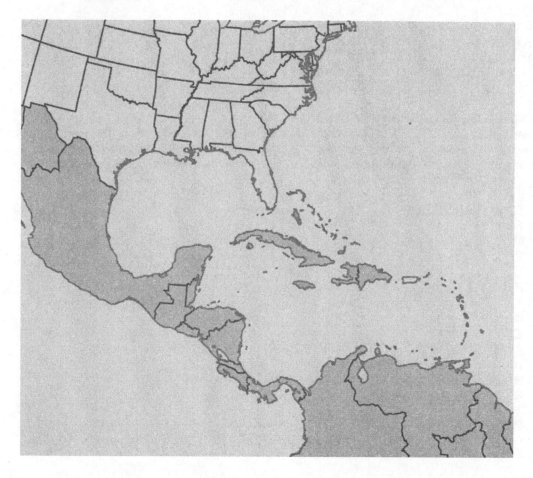

MULTIPLE CHOICE ANSWERS:

1. B (p. 681)
2. E (pp. 681–684)
3. B (p. 682)
4. B (pp. 682–683)
5. D (p. 683)
6. C (p. 683)
7. E (p. 684)
8. A (p. 684)
9. E (p. 685)
10. E (p. 686)

11. D (p. 688)
12. B (p. 689)
13. A (p. 690)
14. A (p. 690)
15. A (p. 691)
16. D (p. 691)
17. B (p. 692)
18. C (p. 692)
19. A (p. 695)
20. E (p. 696)

21. A (p. 697)
22. B (p. 698)
23. B (p. 701)
24. E (p. 702)
25. A (p. 702)

CHRONOLOGICAL ARRANGEMENT ANSWERS:

Seward buys Alaska from Russia, Congress creates Naval Advisory Board, Cleveland rejects annexation of Hawaii, Cubans begin revolt against Spain, Spanish-American War, Filipino-American War begins, Boxer rebellion begins, U.S. acquires Panama Canal Zone, Russo-Japanese War, Panama Canal opens

MATCHING ANSWERS:

1. F
2. M
3. S
4. Q
5. P
6. K
7. D
8. G
9. A
10. H
11. R
12. R
13. T
14. W
15. C

Chapter Twenty-Three
America and the Great War
1914–1920

KEY TOPICS

- **Attempts to Remain Neutral**
- **The War on the Home Front**
- **The War to End Wars in Europe**
- **The Postwar World**

CHAPTER NOTES

In the space below, create your own outline of the chapter. Consider the Key Topics above as well as the overall thrust of the chapter and the text's presentation of material.

Multiple Choice: In the blanks below, write the letter of the **best** response.

1. ____ Which of the following was **not** a contributory cause of the First World War?
   a. Competition among European powers for colonial empires
   b. Precariously balanced European military alliances
   c. The rise of Bolshevism in Russia
   d. German expansionism

2. ____ Which of the following was a member of the Central Powers?
   a. Turkey
   b. Russia
   c. France
   d. Belgium
   e. Italy

3. ____ Which of the following was a member of the Allied Powers?
   a. Germany
   b. Bulgaria
   c. Japan
   d. Austria/Hungary

4. ____ Militarily, World War I was characterized by:
   a. trench warfare and stalemate.
   b. mass slaughter on all fronts.
   c. the introduction of new weaponry.
   d. the abrogation of the "rules" of naval warfare.
   e. all of these things.

5. ____ The United States government and its citizens made every effort to maintain strict neutrality during the early stages of the war.
   a. True
   b. False

6. ____ German submarines began attacking Allied shipping because:
   a. the British were violating international law.
   b. of uneven and superficial American neutrality.
   c. their surface navy was no match for the British navy.
   d. of all of these reasons.
   e. of only b and c.

7. ____ Wilson's attempts to mediate a peaceful resolution in 1917 failed because:
   a. each side had sacrificed too much simply to cease fighting and walk away.
   b. few Europeans were interested in his moralistic preaching.
   c. all sides were interested only in their own national objectives.
   d. of all of these factors.

8. ____ The United States ultimately was drawn into the war militarily in part because of an intercepted message from Germany to:
   a. Russia.
   b. Italy.
   c. France.
   d. Mexico.
   e. Japan.

9. ____ The American people were finally convinced to participate in the war:
   a. by propaganda that depicted Germans as brutal and subhuman.
   b. because Wilson presented the conflict as a great moral crusade.
   c. when Germany offered to give away U.S. territory.
   d. when German submarines began sinking American ships.
   e. because of all of these.

10. ____ As the United States entered the war, most Americans were glad and eager to finally participate.
    a. True
    b. False

11. ____ According to the text, the War Industries Board:
    a. allowed business to amass extraordinary profits.
    b. attempted to micro-manage business and industry.
    c. exhibited a *laissez faire* philosophy.
    d. did all of these things.
    e. only a and b are correct.

12. ____ During America's participation in the war, the role of women remained much as it had been, with women being encouraged to remain at home with their families.
    a. True
    b. False

13. ____ The U.S. government financed the cost of the war by:
    a. borrowing money from banks and wealthy investors.
    b. raising taxes.
    c. selling "Liberty Bonds."
    d. all of these means.

14. ____ The government attempted to maintain popular support for the war by:
    a. barraging the public with pro-war information.
    b. blitzing the public with anti-German propaganda.
    c. stringently suppressing any dissent, even at the cost of civil liberties.
    d. all of these.
    e. only a and b.

15. ____ The "liberty sandwich" became the surrogate name for:
    a. a Reuben sandwich.
    b. a hand grenade.
    c. an American fighter plane.
    d. a hamburger.

16. ____ When the United States entered the Great War, the Allies were:
    a. losing on all fronts.
    b. winning on the western front but losing on the eastern front.
    c. winning on the eastern front but losing on the western front.
    d. winning on land but losing at sea.
    e. winning on all fronts.

17. ____ The "Harlem Hellfighters" were:
    a. an all-black infantry regiment.
    b. the first Allied unit to reach the Rhine.
    c. welcomed as heroes when they returned to the States.
    d. all of these.
    e. only a and b.

18. _____ In Russia, the collapse of the Tsar's regime led to all of the following **except**:
   a. a brief provisional democracy.
   b. the Bolshevik revolution.
   c. a reversal of military momentum on the eastern front.
   d. the freeing of more German troops to fight on the western front.
   e. intervention by British and American troops.

19. _____ American forces achieved military victory at:
   a. Château-Thierry.
   b. Belleau Wood.
   c. Rheims.
   d. Argonne Forest.
   e. all of these places.

20. _____ Woodrow Wilson's Fourteen Points called for all of the following **except**:
   a. national ethnic autonomy in Europe.
   b. international freedom of navigation.
   c. punishment of Germany for its aggression.
   d. the end of secret alliances.
   e. a league of nations pledged to settling world problems peacefully.

21. _____ At Versailles, Britain and France:
   a. heartily endorsed Wilson's Fourteen Points.
   b. viewed Wilson as a self-righteous preacher.
   c. wanted tangible results to show for their years of bloody sacrifice.
   d. did all of these.
   e. did only b and c.

22. _____ Which of the following was **not** represented at the Versailles conference?
   a. Germany
   b. Italy
   c. France
   d. Britain
   e. The United States

23. _____ Though most Americans initially favored the Versailles Treaty, Wilson doomed prospects for America's participation in the League of Nations because:
   a. he had included too many Republicans in the treaty-making process.
   b. he steadfastly refused to compromise.
   c. he failed to campaign for the League vigorously.
   d. his flexibility caused leading Democrats like Bryan to feel betrayed.

24. _____ Following the Great War:
   a. the American economy turned chaotic.
   b. rapidly returning troops caused unemployment and housing shortages.
   c. farm income declined.
   d. women and African Americans failed to realize their prewar hopes.
   e. all of these things happened.

25. _____ In the period of 1919–1921, the term "Red Scare" referred to:
   a. the rise of horror as a motion picture genre.
   b. fears that territory would be returned to Native Americans.
   c. the period between the yellow scare and the blue scare.
   d. heightened security alerts in major U.S. cities.
   e. fears that Bolshevism would spread to the U.S.

Chronological Arrangement: Rearrange the list of events below by **rewriting** each item in correct chronological sequence into the blanks provided.

Sussex Pledge   _____

Bolshevik Revolution in Russia   _____

Peace Conference at Versailles   _____

Armistice ends the Great War   _____

Senate rejects the League of Nations   _____

Wilson suffers a massive stroke   _____

World War I begins in Europe   _____

Woodrow Wilson first elected   _____

U.S. declares war on Germany   _____

Lusitania sunk   _____

Essay: Read each of the following questions, take some time to organize your thoughts, then compose thorough, meaningful answers for each.

1. In what ways did America's participation in World War I reflect attitudes of progressivism?

2. Describe American attitudes toward the war as it was beginning in Europe.

3. In what ways did Americans demonstrate unfair application of neutrality?

4. Discuss how Woodrow Wilson, who "kept us out of war," ultimately involved us in that war.

5. Describe the steps taken by the U.S. government to manage the national economy.

6. How were American women—both black and white—affected by America's participation in the war?

7. Describe how Americans' civil liberties became casualties of the Great War.

8. How did racism affect the experiences of America's black soldiers during the war?

9. In what ways did the participation of the U.S. military change the course of the war?

10. Discuss the harsh settlement imposed upon Germany by the Versailles Treaty.

11. Why did Americans ultimately reject the Treaty of Versailles and its League of Nations?

12. Discuss post-war retrenchment in relations between industry and labor.

13. How and why did the Republicans regain the presidency in 1920?

14. Describe America's efforts to suppress the Bolshevik Revolution.

Matching: Match each description in the left column with the person it most likely describes. (Beware: Not all names will be used!)

1. _____ He kept us out of war, though his one-sided "neutrality" led us into that war

2. _____ Wilson's Sec. of State; tried to urge neutrality, then compromise on the Versailles treaty

3. _____ Supreme Court justice, New York governor; opposed Wilson's reelection in 1916

4. _____ German foreign minister; tried to entice Mexico into the war by promising Texas and Arizona

5. _____ Financier who used the War Industries Board to micromanage U.S. business

6. _____ Organized food relief in Europe, urged Americans to conserve through the Food Administration

7. _____ Hoped that her leadership of the Dept. of Educational Propaganda would lead to women's suffrage

8. _____ Socialist leader, sentenced to prison for suggesting in a speech that free speech was endangered

9. _____ Chased Pancho Villa in Mexico, then led the American Expeditionary Force in France

10. _____ Led Bolsheviks into power and Russia out of the war on the eastern front

11. _____ British Prime Minister; rejected Wilson's preaching, sought his own agenda at Versailles

12. _____ Attorney General who raided suspected radicals, jailed and deported them without trials

13. _____ Weary of great and noble crusades, Americans chose his "normalcy" in the election of 1920

14. _____ Wilson's Assist. Navy Secretary; ran unsuccessfully for Vice President in 1920

15. _____ Tennessee army private; won the Medal of Honor for knocking out 20 Germans and 35 machine guns

A. Albert Burleson

B. Bernard Baruch

C. Carrie Chapman Catt

D. Franklin D. Roosevelt

E. Charles Evans Hughes

F. Robert La Follette

G. Warren G. Harding

H. Herbert Hoover

I. Harold Ickes

J. William J. Bryan

K. Wilhelm II

L. David Lloyd George

M. Mitchell Palmer

N. Neville Chamberlain

O. Vittorio Orlando

P. John J. Pershing

Q. Victoria

R. Ray Stannard Baker

S. Albert Smith

T. Theodore Roosevelt

U. Eugene V. Debs

V. V. I. Lenin

W. Woodrow Wilson

X. James Cox

Y. Alvin York

Z. Arthur Zimmerman

Map Identification: Using the blank map below, locate each of the following items.

Britain	France	Italy
Germany	Austria/Hungary	Russia
Serbia	Bulgaria	Ottoman Empire
Western Front	Eastern Front	

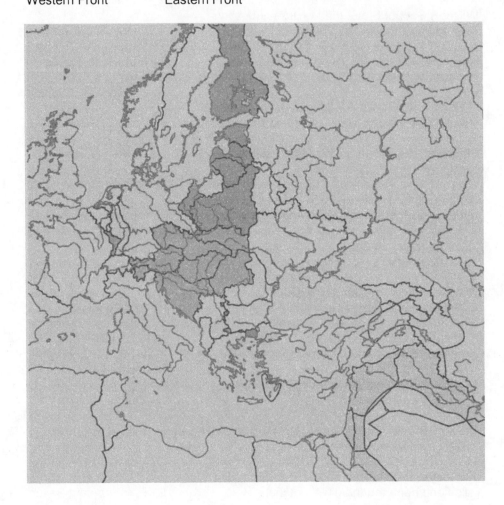

MULTIPLE CHOICE ANSWERS:

1. C (p. 711)
2. A (p. 711)
3. C (p. 711)
4. E (pp. 711–714)
5. B (p. 712)
6. D (pp. 713–714)
7. D (pp. 715–716)
8. D (p. 716)
9. E (pp. 716, 721)
10. B (p. 716)

11. E (p. 717)
12. B (p. 719)
13. D (p. 720)
14. D (p. 721)
15. D (p. 722)
16. A (p. 723)
17. E (p. 723)
18. C (p. 724)
19. E (pp. 723–725)
20. C (p. 725)

21. E (pp. 725–727)
22. A (pp. 726–727)
23. B (p. 731)
24. E (pp. 731–732)
25. E (p. 733)

CHRONOLOGICAL ARRANGEMENT ANSWERS:

Woodrow Wilson first elected, World War I begins in Europe, *Lusitania* sunk, Sussex Pledge, U.S. declares war on Germany, Bolshevik Revolution in Russia, Armistice ends the Great War, Peace Conference at Versailles, Wilson suffers a massive stroke, Senate rejects the League of Nations

MATCHING ANSWERS:

1. W
2. J
3. E
4. Z
5. B
6. H
7. C
8. U
9. P
10. V
11. L
12. M
13. G
14. D
15. Y

Chapter Twenty-Four
Toward a Modern America:
The 1920s

KEY TOPICS

- **The American Economy: Business and Government**
- **The Jazz Age**
- **Beginning the Culture Wars**
- **The United States and World Affairs**

CHAPTER NOTES

In the space below, create your own outline of the chapter. Consider the Key Topics above as well as the overall thrust of the chapter and the text's presentation of material.

Multiple Choice: In the blanks below, write the letter of the **best** response.

1. ____ Which of the following does **not** describe Henry Ford?
   a. He reduced hours and raised wages.
   b. He assailed labor unions.
   c. He welcomed Jewish workers.
   d. He sought to maximize profits and increase efficiency.
   e. He worried about the monotony of the assembly line.

2. ____ What factor(s) spurred the economic boom of the 1920s?
   a. wartime profits
   b. mechanization of business
   c. standardized parts
   d. electricity
   e. all of these answers

3. ____ Which of these industries was stimulated as a result of the coming of the automobile?
   a. steel
   b. rubber
   c. glass
   d. service stations
   e. all of these answers

4. ____ Motion pictures did not enjoy great popularity until sound was introduced in 1929.
   a. True
   b. False

5. ____ Control of an entire industry by a few giant firms is known as
   a. oligarchy.
   b. oligopoly.
   c. monopoly.
   d. vertical integration.
   e. a crying shame.

6. ____ To undercut labor unions and ensure workers' loyalties, some companies
   a. proclaimed open shops.
   b. required yellow-dog contracts.
   c. practiced welfare-capitalism.
   d. offered home financing and stock ownership plans.
   e. all of these answers

7. ____ By the end of the 1920s, most American automobiles were purchased
   a. on credit.
   b. in overseas markets.
   c. only by the upper classes.
   d. by families needing a second vehicle.

8. ____ Which of these industries generally did **not** benefit from the prosperity of the 1920s?
   a. automobile manufacturing
   b. petroleum
   c. agriculture
   d. chemicals
   e. aviation

9. ____ According to the text, the most dynamic office during the Harding administration was the
   a. Oval Office.
   b. State Department.
   c. Commerce Department.
   d. Justice Department.
   e. General Accounting Office.

10. ____ Harding's problems as president stemmed from
   a. his stiff and aloof manner.
   b. his appointment of friends and cronies to office.
   c. his tacit support of racial violence.
   d. his refusal to acknowledge his own limitations.
   e. his refusal to help shape the nation's budget process.

11. ____ The Sheppard-Towner Act was intended to
   a. assist stockmen and ranchers in the West.
   b. grant budget leadership to the president.
   c. provide federal funds for infant and maternity care.
   d. slow the immigration of the Japanese.
   e. stimulate research and development of rocket technology.

12. ____ The "Great Migration" referred to
   a. the move of African Americans away from the South.
   b. the influx of immigrants from southern and eastern Europe.
   c. the swelling of Asian populations on the west coast.
   d. the arrival of persecuted Jews from Russia.
   e. the spread of American jazz into Europe.

13. ____ In the 1920s, the residential and social ideal for most Americans was the
   a. 5th Avenue apartment.
   b. southern, palladian mansion.
   c. single-family house surrounded by a lawn.
   d. Frank Lloyd Wright "prairie house."
   e. mobile home.

14. ____ The first fast-food franchise chain was
   a. Howard Johnson's.
   b. White Castle.
   c. McDonald's.
   d. Kentucky Fried Chicken.
   e. Taco Bell.

15. ____ During the 1920s, advertising transformed the role of the housewife into that of
   a. child bearer.
   b. skilled and savvy consumer.
   c. manufacturer of domestic items.
   d. bread-winner.
   e. cottage industrialist.

16. ____ By the end of the 1920s, most _____ was(were) being bought on credit.
   a. radios
   b. furniture
   c. washing machines
   d. automobiles
   e. all of these answers

17. ____ According to the text, movies such as *The Ten Commandments* and *The King of Kings*
    a. were both passionate and pure.
    b. titillated audiences and reinforced traditional values.
    c. depicted sinful pleasures and the eventual triumph of moral order.
    d. gave the public the sex it wanted while satisfying church groups.
    e. all of these answers

18. ____ American jazz was spread by all of the following **except**
    a. black servicemen in Europe during World War I.
    b. the phonograph.
    c. radio.
    d. television.
    e. the Great Migration.

19. ____ Young women who engaged in fashion fads, dance crazes, smoking, and drinking were called
    a. hussies.
    b. "Gibson girls."
    c. "Harvey girls."
    d. "it girls."
    e. flappers.

20. ____ Writers who rejected the materialism, conformity, and provincialism of mass culture were called
    a. fundamentalists.
    b. the "Lost Generation."
    c. the "Me Generation."
    d. party poopers.
    e. young guns.

21. ____ American-born children of Japanese immigrants were known as "Nisei."
    a. True
    b. False

22. ____ The new Ku Klux Klan of the 1920s was organized for most of the same reasons as the old, post-Civil War Klan.
    a. True
    b. False

23. ____ The "Noble Experiment" referred to an early, failed attempt to fly across the Atlantic.
    a. True
    b. False

24. ____ Anti-liquor laws ultimately
    a. proved easy to evade.
    b. proved impossible to enforce.
    c. funneled huge profits into organized crime.
    d. made small-time hoodlums into millionaires.
    e. all of these answers

25. ____ The fundamentalist champion William Jennings Bryan was also anti-Semitic and anti-Catholic.
    a. True
    b. False

26. _____ Following rejection of the League of Nations, the United States spent the remainder of the 1920s completely disengaged from world affairs.
   a. True
   b. False

27. _____ Following the Great War
   a. American banks lent money to Germany.
   b. Germany used American loan money to pay reparations to Britain and France.
   c. Britain and France used German reparations money to repay American loans.
   d. all of this insanity ensued.
   e. a and b are correct

28. _____ The 1928 Kellogg-Briand Pact
   a. outlawed war.
   b. maintained the "open door" in China.
   c. allowed the U.S. to eliminate "gunboat diplomacy" completely.
   d. reduced naval armaments.
   e. garnered general respect and compliance during the next two decades.

29. _____ Which of the following is **not** true concerning the presidential election of 1928?
   a. Calvin Coolidge did not run.
   b. Republicans ran the more progressive candidate.
   c. The Democratic candidate offered special appeal to the western states.
   d. The results set the stage for political re-alignment in the early 1930s.
   e. The Republicans were still associated with the economic prosperity of the 1920s.

30. _____ Edward Purinton believed that _____ was the salvation of the world.
   a. a return to traditional values
   b. education
   c. technology
   d. family values
   e. business

Chronological Arrangement: Re-arrange the list of events below by re-writing each item in correct chronological sequence into the blanks provided.

Washington Naval Conference   _____

The Great Crash of 1929   _____

Herbert Hoover elected   _____

Warren Harding elected   _____

Teapot Dome Scandal revealed   _____

Charles Lindbergh flies the Atlantic _____

Coolidge assumes the presidency   _____

18th Amendment ratified   _____

Kellogg-Briand Pact outlaws war   _____

Scopes Trial begins   _____

Essay: Read each of the following questions, take some time to organize your thoughts, then compose thorough, meaningful answers for each.

1. Describe Upton Sinclair's view of Henry Ford and how the Great War had changed him.

2. What changes did the automobile bring to American life?

3. Discuss the fate of the labor movement during the 1920s.

4. Why could Herbert Hoover be considered a "bright spot" during the 1920s?

5. What was the effect of the Great Migration upon northern cities? Upon African Americans?

6. In what ways did advertising change Americans' lives?

7. Why could jazz be considered America's most important contribution to the arts?

8. What factors led to changing moral standards and behavior during the 1920s?

9. Discuss the literature of the "Harlem Renaissance" and the "Lost Generation."

10. In what ways did the new Ku Klux Klan of the 1920s differ from the earlier version?

11. Why didn't Prohibition work?

12. Did "fundamentalism" win or lose the Scopes trial?

Matching: Match each description in the left column with the person it most likely describes. (Beware: Not all names will be used. Some may be used more than once!)

1. ____ According to Sinclair, WWI changed him from an innovator to a harsh and draconian businessman.

2. ____ Silent film star who showed his comedic genius in such movies as *The Gold Rush.*

3. ____ Neither capable nor bright, this genial "buddy" appointed buddies who pilfered the public trust.

4. ____ Fed the starving in Europe; as Sec. of Commerce he tried to expand prosperity through efficiency.

5. ____ Only person to serve as both President and Chief Justice of the Supreme Court.

6. ____ Harding's Interior Sec.; went to jail for taking cash for leasing Teapot Dome oil reserves.

7. ____ Vermont Yankee whose calm appearance hid a furious temper and a mean spirit.

8. ____ Jamaican-born New Yorker; black nationalist who urged a back-to-Africa migration.

9. ____ Harlem Renaissance writer whose poetry reflected the rhythm and mood of jazz.

10. ____ Great and trend-setting jazz trumpeter of the 1920s (and '30s, '40s, '50s, and '60s!).

11. ____ The "Sultan of Swat," this baseball immortal's salary was higher than that of the president.

12. ____ In his tiny, home-made airplane, he fought bad weather and fatigue crossing the Atlantic.

13. ____ To movie-goers in the 1920s, she was the "It Girl;" everyone knew what "it" was.

14. ____ In *The Great Gatsby* he described the futility of wealth, but he was self-absorbed as well.

15. ____ His army of almost 1,000 thugs killed hundreds of his competition in Chicago violence.

16. ____ Three-time presidential candidate; condemned anti-Semitism; prosecuted John Scopes.

17. ____ Never elected before, this forgotten progressive and humanitarian was elected president in 1928.

A. Louis Armstrong

B. Clara Bow

C. Calvin Coolidge

D. Clarence Darrow

E. Scott Fitzgerald

F. Warren Harding

G. Herbert Hoover

H. Charles Lindbergh

I. William J. Bryan

J. Robert S. Kerr

K. Langston Hughes

L. H.L. Mencken

M. Al Capone

N. Albert Fall

O. Charlotte Perkins Gilman

P. Vidkung Quisling

Q. George H. ("Babe") Ruth

R. Charlie Chaplin

S. Henry Ford

T. Upton Sinclair

U. Marcus Garvey

V. William H. Taft

W. Alfred E. Smith

X. Harry Daugherty

Y. Zora Neale Hurston

MULTIPLE CHOICE ANSWERS:

1. C (pp. 740–741)
2. E (pp. 741–742)
3. E (p. 742)
4. B (p. 742)
5. B (p. 743)
6. E (p. 743)
7. A (p. 744)
8. C (p. 745)
9. C (p. 746)
10. B (p. 747)

11. C (pp. 749–750)
12. A (p. 750)
13. C (p. 753)
14. B (p. 753)
15. B (p. 754)
16. E (pp. 744, 754)
17. E (p. 754)
18. D (pp. 754–756)
19. E (p. 756)
20. B (p. 757)

21. A (p. 759)
22. B (p. 759)
23. B (p. 760)
24. E (p. 760)
25. B (p. 761)
26. B (p. 761)
27. D (p. 762)
28. A (p. 762)
29. C (p. 763)
30. E (p. 748)

CHRONOLOGICAL ARRANGEMENT ANSWERS:

18th Amendment ratified, Warren Harding elected, Washington Naval Conference, Teapot Dome Scandal revealed, Coolidge assumes the presidency, Scopes Trial begins, Charles Lindbergh flies the Atlantic, Kellogg-Briand Pact outlaws war, Herbert Hoover elected, The Great Crash of 1929

MATCHING ANSWERS:

1. S
2. R
3. F
4. G
5. V
6. N
7. C
8. U
9. K
10. A
11. Q
12. H
13. B
14. E
15. M
16. I
17. G

Chapter Twenty-Five
The Great Depression and the New Deal
1929–1939

KEY TOPICS

- The Stock Market Crash and its Effects
- The New Deal: Its Goals, Effects, and Challenges
- Foreign Policy and the Prelude to War

CHAPTER NOTES

In the space below, create your own outline of the chapter. Consider the Key Topics above as well as the overall thrust of the chapter and the text's presentation of material.

Multiple Choice: In the blanks below, write the letter of the **best** response.

1. _____ According to the text, unemployed Americans liked the Roosevelts because
   a. they had come from similar, humble backgrounds.
   b. they promised to replace capitalism with socialism.
   c. they believed the Roosevelts actually cared about their plight.
   d. all of these answers

2. _____ Federal activism of the 1930s
   a. achieved full economic recovery.
   b. affected systematic reform.
   c. restored Americans' confidence.
   d. transformed the nation's responsibilities to its citizens.
   e. both c and d

3. _____ Which of the following did **not** contribute to the onset of the Great Depression?
   a. insufficient consumer purchasing power
   b. declining agricultural production and resulting high commodity prices
   c. government's *laissez faire* policies
   d. oligopolies that dominated national wealth
   e. international debt and reparations payments following World War I

4. _____ American families during the depression experienced all of the following **except**
   a. skyrocketing divorce rates.
   b. husbands deserting their families.
   c. declining birthrates.
   d. increased female-headed households.
   e. increased home production of food and clothing.

5. _____ Many Hispanic families
   a. avoided seeking monetary relief and health care.
   b. faced competition from displaced whites who now wanted their low-paying jobs.
   c. feared deportation.
   d. were driven out of the southwestern United States.
   e. all of these answers

6. _____ Herbert Hoover's initial response to the deepening depression was to
   a. "feel our pain."
   b. compose the song "We Are the World."
   c. wait for the economy to turn around on its own.
   d. rely on individual and voluntary private relief.
   e. both c and d

7. _____ Despite his admirable record as a brilliant engineer, humanitarian, and visionary Secretary of Commerce, Hoover was seen by depression-weary Americans as
   a. indifferent to their suffering.
   b. magnanimous even in his hollow gestures.
   c. unwilling to try anything to restore buying power.
   d. callous toward the needs of businesses and their employees.

8. _____ Overall, most Americans were pleased that Douglas McArthur was able to quell the embarrassing spectacle of the "Bonus Army."
   a. True
   b. False

9. _____ During the presidential campaign of 1932, Franklin Roosevelt spelled out specific, step-by-step plans for dealing with the depression.
   a. True
   b. False

10. _____ Which of the following was **not** a source of ideas for FDR's New Deal?
   a. academic experts
   b. the "brain trust"
   c. Upton Sinclair's socialism
   d. progressive principles
   e. Herbert Hoover

11. _____ After his inauguration, FDR immediately shut down the nation's
   a. railroad system.
   b. banking system.
   c. postal system.
   d. movie industry.
   e. steel industry.

12. _____ One of FDR's most effective ways to calm Americans' fears was through
   a. irresponsible promises.
   b. fireside chats.
   c. press conferences.
   d. donating his family's personal fortune.

13. _____ The new Social Security system lacked
   a. unemployment compensation.
   b. old-age pensions.
   c. aid for dependent mothers.
   d. health insurance.
   e. a regressive payroll tax.

14. _____ Which of the following groups had **not** become part of the Democratic/Roosevelt coalition by 1936?
   a. white southern racists
   b. western farmers
   c. members of labor unions
   d. wealthy Americans
   e. urban ethnic groups

15. _____ The Committee (later Congress) of Industrial Organizations unionized
   a. steel workers.
   b. auto workers.
   c. rubber workers.
   d. black workers.
   e. all of these groups

16. _____ Most New Deal agencies proved to be a great benefit for American women, both white and black.
   a. True
   b. False

17. _____ The plight of African Americans improved considerably during the New Deal because FDR was not afraid to stand up to southern white Democrats.
   a. True
   b. False

18. ____ The Indian Reorganization Act of 1934 (the "Indian New Deal")
    a. guaranteed religious freedom for Native People.
    b. re-established tribal government.
    c. halted the sale of tribal lands.
    d. promoted tribal businesses.
    e. all of these answers

19. ____ Roosevelt's "court packing" scheme would have allowed him to appoint
    a. 15 justices.
    b. 6 justices.
    c. 9 justices.
    d. 10 justices.
    e. a new justice to replace each one serving past the age of 70.

20. ____ By the 1930s, Americans had become _____ with their World War I experience.
    a. euphoric
    b. content
    c. disillusioned
    d. bored
    e. satisfied

21. ____ Extending formal diplomatic recognition to the Soviet Union in 1933 led to immediate trade opportunities for American companies.
    a. True
    b. False

22. ____ Concerning Latin America, FDR
    a. extended Hoover's "Good Neighbor" policy.
    b. ordered the removal of all U.S. troops in the hemisphere.
    c. frequently authorized intervention to restore order in several countries.
    d. refused to support a Cuban coup.
    e. rejected all invitations to leave the country while in office.

23. ____ Which of the following was not a fascist dictator?
    a. Benito Mussolini
    b. Adolf Hitler
    c. Francisco Franco
    d. Neville Chamberlain

24. ____ The term "*Kristallnacht*" refers to
    a. the twelfth day of Christmas.
    b. the "night of broken glass."
    c. Hitler's violent pogrom against Jews.
    d. a German harvest festival.
    e. both b and c

25. ____ According to John Collier, "Indian-ness" is rooted in
    a. land.
    b. tribal consciousness.
    c. Native religion.
    d. racial features.
    e. blood quantum.

Chronological Arrangement: Re-arrange the list of events below by re-writing each item in correct chronological sequence into the blanks provided.

Indian Reorganization Act   _____

FDR first elected president   _____

Pearl Harbor attacked   _____

Hitler "appeased" at Munich   _____

Japan invades Manchuria   _____

FDR begins unprecedented third term _____

Hitler assumes power in Germany   _____

Stock market crashes   _____

Supreme Court strikes down the NRA _____

FDR's "hundred days"   _____

Essay: Read each of the following questions, take some time to organize your thoughts, then compose thorough, meaningful answers for each.

1. The stock market crash did not cause the depression. What did?

2. In what ways were women's jobs more secure in the 1930s? How were they *less* secure?

3. Why were African Americans hit especially hard by the Depression?

254

4. Discuss President Hoover's response to the depression. Why did it prove inadequate?

5. Describe Franklin Roosevelt's New Deal philosophy. Would you consider it Liberal? Conservative? Pragmatic?

6. Who were FDR's chief critics? What did they want?

7. Explain why FDR believed he needed to "pack" the Supreme Court.

8. In what ways did FDR shift his emphasis away from domestic concerns in the late 1930s?

9. What are some of the most important legacies of the New Deal?

Matching: Match each description in the left column with the person it most likely describes. (Beware: Not all names will be used. Some may be used more than once!)

1. _____ His wait-and-see volunteerism proved inadequate in suppressing the depression.

2. _____ Suppressed the "Bonus Army' with cavalry, infantry, and even tanks.

3. _____ Harvard-trained only son of a patrician New York family; distant cousin of the 26th President.

4. _____ FDR's chief administrator of relief; became director of the FERA.

5. _____ PWA director, he spent billions to build schools, hospitals, courthouses, dams, and bridges.

6. _____ Head of the United Mine Workers; he applauded creation of the Recovery Administration.

7. _____ California physician whose 5,000 clubs lobbied to help the elderly poor.

8. _____ Anti-Semitic Catholic priest who used weekly radio broadcasts to demand social justice.

9. _____ His "share-the-wealth" program offered to pay poor Americans by taxing the wealthy at 90%.

10. _____ His landmark legislation gave workers the right to organize and to bargain collectively.

11. _____ Member of the "brain trust," he pushed to resettle farmers on better land.

12. _____ Moved from FERA to WPA, which built most of the nation's surviving infrastructure.

13. _____ Unlucky Republican challenger in 1936, was buried in the worst landslide election ever.

14. _____ As Secretary of Labor, she became the first female cabinet member.

15. _____ The "cabinet member without portfolio," she was her husband's eyes, ears, and often conscience.

16. _____ Social worker who championed rehabilitation of Native American economy and culture.

17. _____ British economist who advocated deficit spending to boost demand and therefore consumption.

18. _____ Senator whose committee both reflected and shaped American attitudes toward WWI (and WWII).

A. Alf Landon

B. Fulgencio Batista

C. Father Charles Coughlin

D. Franklin D. Roosevelt

E. Eleanor Roosevelt

F. Francisco Franco

G. John Kenneth Galbraith

H. Harry Hopkins

I. Harold Ickes

J. John Collier

K. John Maynard Keynes

L. John L. Lewis

M. Douglas MacArthur

N. Gerald Nye

O. Herbert Hoover

P. Frances Perkins

Q. Elizabeth II

R. Walter Rauschenbusch

S. Henry Stimson

T. Francis Townsend

U. Huey Long

V. Arthur Vandenburgh

W. Robert Wagner

X. Rexford Tugwell

Y. Yuri Gagarin

Z. Arthur Zimmermann

Matching: Match each description in the left column with the New Deal agency most closely associated with that description. (Some may be used twice, others not at all.)

1. ____ Safeguarded bank deposits up to $2,000   A. AAA

2. ____ Regulated stock market speculation   B. NRA

3. ____ Furnished money to state and local agencies   C. CCC

4. ____ Combined relief with forestation and flood control   D. FDIC

5. ____ Paid farmers to restrict production   E. SEC

6. ____ Established business codes, prices, wages   F. FERA

7. ____ Unemployment compensation, old-age pensions   G. Soc. Sec.

8. ____ Employed writers, artists, musicians, actors, builders   H. TVA

9. ____ Gave part-time jobs to students   I. NLRB

10. ____ Urged consumers to buy from participating companies   J. WPA

11. ____ Gave workers the right to organize and bargain   K. MIC

12. ____ Spent $12 billion, employing 1/5 of the labor force   L. KEY

13. ____ Employed southerners to build hydroelectric dams   M. OUS

14. ____ Extended power lines through non-profit cooperatives   N. NYA

15. ____ Built dams to control southern flooding   O. REA

MULTIPLE CHOICE ANSWERS:

1. C (p. 773)
2. E (p. 773)
3. B (pp. 774–776)
4. A (p. 779)
5. E (pp. 780–781)
6. E (pp. 781–782)
7. A (p. 782)
8. B (p. 782)
9. B (p. 783)
10. C (p. 783)

11. B (p. 784)
12. B (p. 784)
13. D (p. 790)
14. D (pp. 791–792)
15. E (p. 793)
16. B (p. 793)
17. B (p. 794)
18. E (p. 795)
19. A (p. 798)
20. C (p. 799)

21. B (p. 799)
22. A (p. 799)
23. D (p. 799)
24. E (pp. 800–801)
25. A (p. 787)

CHRONOLOGICAL ARRANGEMENT ANSWERS:

Stock market crashes, Japan invades Manchuria, FDR first elected president, FDR's "100 Days", Hitler assumes power in Germany, Indian Reorganization Act, Supreme Court strikes down the NRA, Hitler "appeased" at Munich, FDR begins unprecedented third term, Pearl Harbor attacked

MATCHING ANSWERS:

1. O
2. M
3. D
4. H
5. I
6. L
7. T
8. C
9. U
10. W
11. X
12. H
13. A
14. P
15. E
16. J
17. K
18. N

MATCHING ANSWERS:

1. D
2. E
3. F
4. C
5. A
6. B
7. G
8. J
9. N
10. B
11. I
12. J
13. H
14. O
15. H

Chapter Twenty-Six
World War II
1939–1945

KEY TOPICS

- **Attempts to Remain Neutral**
- **Moving toward War**
- **The War in Europe**
- **The War in the Pacific**
- **Victory Indeed**

CHAPTER NOTES

In the space below, create your own outline of the chapter. Consider the Key Topics above as well as the overall thrust of the chapter and the text's presentation of material.

Multiple Choice: In the blanks below, write the letter of the **best** response.

1. _____ The root causes of World War II included all of the following **except**:
   a. European economic hardship and political instability.
   b. Japanese racist appeal to Japanese pride.
   c. Hitler's racist appeal to Germans' pride.
   d. Americans' desire to end the depression, even by war if necessary.
   e. World War I.

2. _____ Hitler's (and Germans') principal territorial desire was to expand into:
   a. eastern Europe.
   b. France.
   c. northern Africa.
   d. Italy.
   e. the Balkans and Greece.

3. _____ Hitler's invasion technique, involving dive bombers, tanks, and motorized infantry, was known as:
   a. "*Kristallnacht.*"
   b. "*Lebensraum.*"
   c. "*Blitzkrieg.*"
   d. "*Luftwaffe.*"
   e. "*Unterseeboot.*"

4. _____ By 1940, Franklin Roosevelt's main interest in the war was to:
   a. support Britain and China.
   b. commit American troops into combat as quickly as possible.
   c. appease Hitler by giving up small portions of European territory.
   d. allow Japan to keep Manchuria, but not China.
   e. prepare for an attack on Hawaii.

5. _____ Even before war was declared in December of 1941, the U.S. was engaged in open combat in:
   a. the North Atlantic.
   b. the South Pacific.
   c. the English Channel.
   d. northern Africa.
   e. France.

6. _____ Roosevelt and Winston Churchill issued their first joint statement of war goals:
   a. at Tehran.
   b. at Yalta.
   c. in the Atlantic Charter.
   d. in the Lend-Lease Act.
   e. immediately after FDR's successful reelection in 1940.

7. _____ According to the text, American moves were intended to be:
   a. aggressive but measured in the Atlantic.
   b. firm but defensive in the Pacific.
   c. deliberately provocative in the Pacific.
   d. deliberately antagonistic in Europe.
   e. both a and b.

8. _____ During the attack at Pearl Harbor, Japanese planes destroyed all of the following **except**:
   a. eight battleships.
   b. two aircraft carriers.
   c. nearly all military aircraft on the island of Oahu.
   d. storage and repair facilities.
   e. both b and d.

9. _____ Which of the following was **not** one of the major fronts in World War II?
   a. The Eastern Front
   b. The North Atlantic
   c. North Africa
   d. The South Atlantic
   e. The "CBI" (China/Burma/India) theater

10. _____ According to the text, the turning point of the war in Europe came at:
   a. Stalingrad.
   b. El Alamein.
   c. Sicily.
   d. Normandy.
   e. Bastogne.

11. _____ The Allies finally gained control in the North Atlantic because:
   a. their aircraft began tracking submarines with radar.
   b. aircraft and surface vessels began using depth charges.
   c. new sonar systems were developed to track U-boats.
   d. new American ships were built at an amazing pace.
   e. of all of these factors.

12. _____ The German advance in North Africa was halted and reversed at:
   a. El Alamein.
   b. Tunisia.
   c. Algiers.
   d. the Suez Canal.
   e. Rick's *Café Americain* in Casablanca.

13. _____ At Midway, three state-of-the-art Japanese aircraft carriers were destroyed in:
   a. 5 minutes.
   b. 5 hours.
   c. 24 hours.
   d. 3 days.
   e. 6 months.

14. _____ The United States was able to out-produce its enemies because:
   a. its population was greater.
   b. a smaller percentage of the population was active in the military.
   c. it applied mass-production techniques to aircraft and ship building.
   d. the U.S. was fighting only a single-front war.
   e. the government required all Americans to contribute to industrial production.

15. _____ As a result of the war effort:
   a. some people became very wealthy.
   b. overall per capita income doubled.
   c. farm income finally overcame its decades-long slump.
   d. southern and western cities increased in size and importance.
   e. all of these phenomena happened.

16. _____ Which of the following cities was **not** involved in the Manhattan Project?
   a. Chicago, Illinois
   b. Los Alamos, New Mexico
   c. Oak Ridge, Tennessee
   d. Boston, Massachusetts
   e. Richland, Washington

17. _____ About how many American service men and women were killed in battle in World War II?
   a. 5,000
   b. 58,000
   c. 115,000
   d. 290,000
   e. 600,000

18. _____ During the war, more than 300 Navajos:
   a. were used to send smoke signals.
   b. refused to surrender at Bastogne.
   c. created symbolic sand paintings to boost morale.
   d. transmitted information in their native language.
   e. planted the U.S. flag on Iwo Jima.

19. _____ For the first time in American military history, black soldiers were treated as equals in combat units.
   a. True
   b. False

20. _____ During the war, marriage rates:
   a. declined, because women were afraid that combat would claim their husbands.
   b. declined, due to a rise in casual romances between people constantly being moved around by the war.
   c. increased, because men and women were trying to "beat the clock."
   d. increased, because of women trying to become eligible for military allotments.
   e. retained the stagnant rate seen during the depression.

21. _____ During the war, most Native Americans tended to remain on reservations to support the war effort through "cottage industries."
   a. True
   b. False

22. _____ During the war, Franklin Roosevelt continued to ignore the plight of African Americans as he had often done during the depression.
   a. True
   b. False

23. _____ Attire with long, wide-shouldered jackets and pleated, narrow-cuffed trousers were known as:
   a. leisure suits.
   b. latino suits.
   c. monkey suits.
   d. zoot suits.
   e. birthday suits.

24. ____ Most Japanese-Americans harbored secret hopes for the success of the Japanese military against the United States.
   a. True.
   b. False.

25. ____ Which was not the site of a war-time meeting between the major Allied leaders?
   a. Casablanca
   b. Tehran
   c. Geneva
   d. Yalta
   e. Potsdam

26. ____ Hitler's last, desperate offensive was called:
   a. the Battle of the Bulge.
   b. Operation Overlord.
   c. the Final Solution.
   d. *Winzigkrieg.*

27. ____ The war in the Pacific theater was characterized by:
   a. racial hatred on both sides.
   b. an island-hopping campaign.
   c. ferocious defense by Japanese of their outer islands.
   d. firebombing of Japanese cities.
   e. all of these.

28. ____ The main reason(s) the U.S. opted to drop atomic bombs on Japan was (were):
   a. retaliation for Pearl Harbor.
   b. racist assumptions about Japanese inferiority.
   c. to hasten the end of the war.
   d. to avoid the necessity of an invasion bloodbath.
   e. both c and d.

29. ____ The nation that lost the greatest number of casualties—military and civilian—in World War II was:
   a. Japan.
   b. Germany.
   c. Russia.
   d. the United States.
   e. China.

30. ____ At the end of the war, most Americans' attitudes and emotions consisted of all of the following **except**:
   a. relief—that the long conflict was finally over.
   b. disillusionment—about our participation in another European war.
   c. anxiousness—about a possible future conflict with the Soviets.
   d. unified—by their shared wartime efforts.

Chronological Arrangement: Rearrange the list of events below by **rewriting** each item in correct chronological sequence into the blanks provided.

Hitler becomes German Chancellor _____

Italy invades Ethiopia _____

Peace Conference at Versailles _____

Japan invades China _____

Spanish Civil War _____

Pearl Harbor attacked _____

Germany invades Poland _____

Battle of Britain _____

Japan invades Manchuria _____

Munich Conference _____

Chronological Arrangement: Rearrange the list of events below by **rewriting** each item in correct chronological sequence into the blanks provided.

Japanese defeated at Midway _____

Japan surrenders in Tokyo Bay _____

"Big Three" meet at Yalta _____

D-Day invasion at Normandy _____

FDR dies; Truman becomes president _____

Pearl Harbor attacked _____

Hiroshima bombed _____

Germany surrenders _____

Battle of the Bulge _____

U.S. and Britain invade Italy _____

Essay: Read each of the following questions, take some time to organize your thoughts, then compose thorough, meaningful answers for each.

1. What was the appeal of Adolf Hitler to the German people? Would he have been believed or accepted if times had been better in 1930s Germany?

2. Why were Americans reluctant to engage in another European war? What did they hope would happen?

3. Explain how relations between the U.S. and Japan deteriorated prior to December 7, 1941.

4. How did the Russian people avoid military defeat by the German army?

5. Discuss the reasons why the majority of Americans supported the war effort in the 1940s.

6. How did average Americans fight World War II at home?

7. How did the national media cover World War II, compared with their handling of recent wars?

8. Why were Japanese-Americans singled out for harsher treatment than that imposed on German-Americans or Italian-Americans?

9. Describe how Hitler's anti-Semitism went from bad to worse to tragic.

10. List and discuss the reasons underlying the decision to use nuclear weapons against Japan.

11. Why did the Allies win World War II?

12. In what ways did World War II change America irrevocably?

Map Identification: Using the blank map below, locate each of the following items.

Vichy France   Leningrad   London
El Alamein   Stalingrad   Paris
Rome   Moscow   Berlin
Normandy   Kursk   Dresden
Norway   Battle of the Bulge

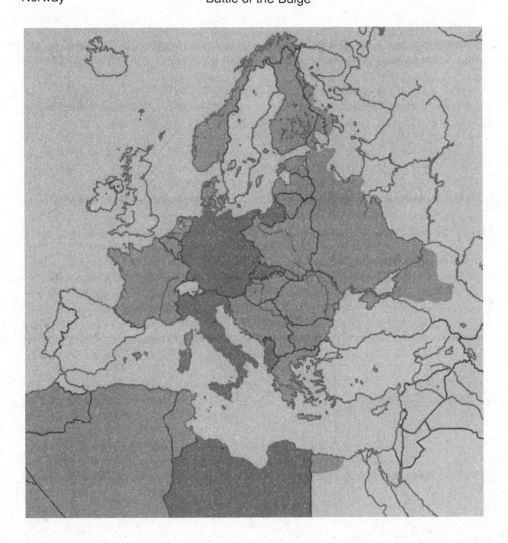

Map Identification: Using the blank map below, locate each of the following items.

Manchuria	Midway	Iwo Jima
Singapore	Tarawa	Hiroshima
Aleutian Islands	Leyte Gulf	Nagasaki
Pearl Harbor	Okinawa	Tokyo

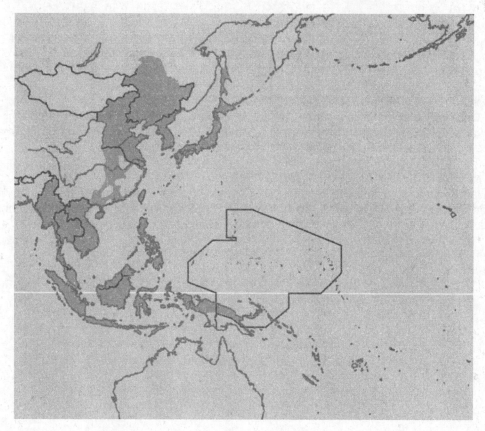

MULTIPLE CHOICE ANSWERS:

1. D (pp. 809–810)	11. E (pp. 818–819)	21. B (p. 826)
2. A (p. 810)	12. A (p. 819)	22. B (p. 826)
3. C (p. 811)	13. A (p. 820)	23. D (p. 826)
4. A (p. 813)	14. C (p. 821)	24. B (pp. 826–827)
5. A (p. 814)	15. E (pp. 821–822)	25. C (pp. 829, 836)
6. C (p. 814)	16. D (p. 823)	26. A (p. 833)
7. E (p. 814)	17. D (p. 823)	27. E (pp. 834–836)
8. E (p. 815)	18. D (pp. 823–824)	28. E (pp. 836–837)
9. D (p. 817)	19. B (p. 824)	29. C (p. 838)
10. A (p. 817)	20. C (p. 824)	30. B (p. 838)

CHRONOLOGICAL ARRANGEMENT ANSWERS:

Peace Conference at Versailles, Japan invades Manchuria, Hitler becomes German Chancellor, Italy invades Ethiopia, Spanish Civil War, Japan invades China, Munich Conference, Germany invades Poland, Battle of Britain, Pearl Harbor attacked

CHRONOLOGICAL ARRANGEMENT ANSWERS:

Pearl Harbor attacked, Japanese defeated at Midway, U.S. and Britain invade Italy, D-Day invasion at Normandy, Battle of the Bulge, "Big Three" meet at Yalta, FDR dies; Truman becomes president, Germany surrenders, Hiroshima bombed, Japan surrenders in Tokyo Bay

Chapter Twenty-Seven
The Cold War at Home and Abroad
1946–1952

KEY TOPICS

- **The Postwar Economic Boom**
- **Truman's Centrist Politics**
- **The Many Fronts of the Cold War**

CHAPTER NOTES

In the space below, create your own outline of the chapter. Consider the Key Topics above as well as the overall thrust of the chapter and the text's presentation of material.

Multiple Choice: In the blanks below, write the letter of the **best** response.

1. _____ The award-winning film *The Best Years of Our Lives* chronicles:
   a. an infantry company during the D-Day invasion.
   b. the devastation inflicted upon Hiroshima.
   c. the postwar adjustment of returning servicemen.
   d. three families' move to postwar suburbia.
   e. America's entry into the Korean War.

2. _____ In the months after the end of World War II, the U.S. experienced all of the following **except**:
   a. the slow release of 12 million veterans.
   b. shortages of consumer goods.
   c. strikes in essential industries.
   d. food shortages.
   e. rising employment tied to consumer demand.

3. _____ The 1947 Taft-Hartley Act:
   a. barred the "closed shop."
   b. blocked secondary boycotts.
   c. imposed a cooling-off period to postpone strikes.
   d. accomplished all of these.
   e. did only a and c.

4. _____ The GI Bill of Rights:
   a. encouraged veterans to pursue home ownership.
   b. encouraged veterans to skip college and find immediate employment.
   c. maintained university education as the preserve of the well-to-do.
   d. increased the percentage of women in college classrooms.
   e. accomplished all of these.

5. _____ The first "Levittown" was built:
   a. near Cincinnati.
   b. on Long Island.
   c. near Chicago.
   d. near Dallas.
   e. near Los Angeles.

6. _____ The American war that finally began to open doors of opportunity for black servicemen was:
   a. World War I.
   b. World War II.
   c. Korea.
   d. Vietnam.
   e. Desert Storm.

7. _____ Hollywood's most typical portrayal of women in the 1950s was that of:
   a. independent career women.
   b. helpless victims.
   c. seductive vixens.
   d. social crusaders.
   e. government secret agents.

8. _____ Successful Democratic candidates in the 1950s had to:
   a. appeal to their liberal base by appearing open to socialist reforms.
   b. appear tough on communism in order to enact domestic reforms.
   c. renounce the socialist philosophies and programs of the New Deal.
   d. avoid being seen as a wishy-washy centrist.

9. _____ The presidential campaign of 1948 was unique in that:
   a. it was the last time a major candidate crisscrossed the nation by train.
   b. it was the first time national television broadcast the two party conventions.
   c. it produced what was likely the first advertising T-shirt.
   d. public opinion pollsters assumed a finish different than the actual outcome.
   e. all of these were features.

10. _____ Harry Truman, through his "Fair Deal," promised to:
   a. replace the New Deal with different programs.
   b. extend the New Deal through additional programs.
   c. end all New Deal programs immediately.
   d. leave all New Deal programs exactly as they were.
   e. transfer all New Deal programs to state and local control.

11. _____ From a historical perspective, the Russian people had no legitimate cause to fear the United States.
   a. True
   b. False

12. _____ Both sides during the Cold War tended to regard the world political situation:
   a. as a series of "either-or" choices.
   b. in "black vs. white" terms.
   c. with an "us-against-them" mentality.
   d. with vulnerability and fear.
   e. in all of these ways.

13. _____ The "Truman Doctrine" was prompted by events in:
   a. Korea.
   b. Southeast Asia.
   c. Poland.
   d. Czechoslovakia.
   e. Greece.

14. _____ Which of the following nations did not come under Soviet domination during the years after World War II?
   a. Poland
   b. Czechoslovakia
   c. Hungary
   d. Austria
   e. Bulgaria

15. _____ The position paper known as NSC-68:
   a. tended to reflect George Kennan's assessment of Soviet aims.
   b. described a world divided between "slavery" and "freedom."
   c. assumed the Soviet Union was motivated by territorial greed and fanatical communism.
   d. did all of these.
   e. did only b and c.

16. _____ The Korean War was all of the following **except**:
   a. an outgrowth of a Korean civil war.
   b. fueled by Soviet equipment and Chinese training.
   c. officially a United Nations action.
   d. a true multi-national coalition.
   e. a repudiation of Kennan's Containment philosophy.

17. _____ The Korean War ended:
   a. in a military stalemate.
   b. after months of stalled negotiations.
   c. with almost the same geographic division as when the war started.
   d. with all of these.
   e. with a and b only.

18. _____ The "Hollywood Ten":
   a. consisted of screenwriters and directors.
   b. refused to discuss their past political associations.
   c. relied on the First Amendment to rescue them.
   d. ultimately went to jail.
   e. experienced all of these.

19. _____ Joseph McCarthy asserted that that communists had infiltrated:
   a. the State Department.
   b. the Defense Department.
   c. the Army.
   d. everything.

20. _____ According to the text, Americans were actually more secure from international threats during the Cold War than they realized.
   a. True
   b. False

Chronological Arrangement: Rearrange the list of events below by **rewriting** each item in correct chronological sequence into the blanks provided.

U.S. tests hydrogen bomb   _____

Rosenbergs convicted of spying   _____

Joseph McCarthy speaks in Wheeling _____

Marshall Plan begins   _____

Berlin Airlift begins   _____

Korean War begins   _____

Soviet Union tests an atomic bomb _____

United Nations established   _____

Winston Churchill's "Iron Curtain" speech _____

China "falls" to Mao Zedong   _____

Essay: Read each of the following questions, take some time to organize your thoughts, then compose thorough, meaningful answers for each.

1. Describe America's brief economic trouble at the close of World War II. What reversed the situation?

2. What means were used to exclude African Americans from suburban America after the war?

3. How did the "Baby Boom" develop? What were its implications in society?

4. What tactics did Harry Truman employ to portray the 80th Congress as "do-nothing"?

5. What happened during the Truman administration to transform the Social Security system?

6. Why and how did both sides of the Cold War view the other with such suspicion?

7. Why was 1949 such a traumatic year for Americans during the early Cold War?

8. Why did President Truman relieve Douglas MacArthur of command in Korea?

9. Describe the series of American miscalculations and missteps that caused the Korean adventure to end the way it did.

10. Why was Hollywood a prime target for those seeking to root out communist sympathizers?

11. Explain the psychological phenomenon known as "McCarthyism."

12. Overall, was the United States better or worse during the Truman years? Explain your opinions.

Matching: Match each description in the left column with the person it most likely describes. (Beware: Not all names will be used. Some may be used more than once!)

1. _____ Loved (and hated) head of the United Mine Workers, blamed for most post-war labor problems.

2. _____ Built thousands of 800 sq ft, 2 BR, 1 BA, LR "assembly-line" houses for VA/FHA Americans.

3. _____ Often-segregated but artful Brooklyn Dodger who opened major league baseball for minorities forever.

4. _____ Artful Missouri pragmatist; his appeal to the "vital center" defined Democratic politics for decades.

5. _____ Seen by most voters as a kook, he was supported by Progressives and Communists in 1948.

6. _____ South Carolina "Dixiecrat" who masked racism behind a façade of "states' rights."

7. _____ Snobbish, arrogant governor of New York; belittled western towns as "whistle stops" in 1948.

8. _____ "Gave 'em Hell," by surprising pollsters with his election recovery in late October 1948.

9. _____ Business tycoon who may have been the first to characterize U.S./Soviet relations as a "cold war."

10. _____ Diplomat whose "long telegram" and anonymous article recommended a U.S. "containment" policy.

11. _____ In Missouri, he suggested that an "iron curtain" had descended from the Baltic to the Black Seas.

12. _____ His Doctrine pledged U.S. support to help nations resist internal subversion or external aggression.

13. _____ His plan created an "empire by invitation" by meeting Europe's economic needs and stifling communism.

14. _____ Post-war dictator in Japan, his enormous ego led to clouded judgment and stalemate in Korea.

15. _____ His communist troops drove Jiang Jieshi to Taiwan, established the "Peoples' Republic" in China.

16. _____ Had to be relieved of command to be reminded who the Commander-in-Chief is supposed to be.

17. _____ Member of the hated "East-coast" establishment; probably passed information to the Soviets.

18. _____ "Tail gunner" whose reckless accusations despite lack of evidence finally brought him down.

A. Douglas MacArthur

B. Bernard Baruch

C. Winston Churchill

D. Thomas Dewey

E. Ethel Rosenberg

F. François Mitterand

G. George Patton

H. Alger Hiss

I. Henry A. Wallace

J. Joseph McCarthy

K. George Kennan

L. John L. Lewis

M. George C. Marshall

N. Ho Chi Minh

O. Jesse Owens

P. Elvis Presley

Q. Elizabeth I

R. Jackie Robinson

S. Strom Thurmond

T. Harry Truman

U. John Updike

V. Arthur Vandenburg

W. William Levitt

X. Richard Nixon

Y. Syngman Rhee

Z. Mao Zedong

Matching: Match each description in the left column with the agency or organization it most likely describes.

1. _____ Encouraged veterans to attend college   A. ANZUS

2. _____ Initiated anti-segregation lawsuits   B. World Bank

3. _____ Stabilized national currencies   C. CIA

4. _____ Gave loans from strong governments to weak ones   D. AEC

5. _____ Handled intelligence gathering and covert operations   E. NATO

6. _____ Assembled top diplomatic and military advisors   F. NAACP

7. _____ Secured deployment of U.S. troops in western Europe   G. GI Bill

8. _____ Civilian-controlled nuclear regulation   H. HUAC

9. _____ Pact between Australia, New Zealand, and the U.S.   I. IMF

10. _____ Investigated anti-U.S. propaganda   J. NSC

MULTIPLE CHOICE ANSWERS:

1. C (p. 844)
2. A (p. 845)
3. D (p. 846)
4. A (p. 846)
5. B (p. 847)
6. B (p. 848)
7. B (p. 850)
8. B (p. 851)
9. E (p. 852)
10. B (p. 852)

11. B (pp. 853–854)
12. E (pp. 853–854)
13. E (p. 855)
14. D (p. 856)
15. D (pp. 855–856, 859)
16. E (pp. 860–861)
17. D (p. 862)
18. E (p. 865)
19. D (pp. 867–868)
20. A (p. 869)

CHRONOLOGICAL ARRANGEMENT ANSWERS:

United Nations established, Winston Churchill's "Iron Curtain" speech, Marshall Plan begins, Berlin Airlift begins, China "falls" to Mao Zedong, Soviet Union tests an atomic bomb, Joseph McCarthy speaks in Wheeling, Korean War begins, Rosenbergs convicted of spying, U.S. tests hydrogen bomb

MATCHING ANSWERS: **MATCHING ANSWERS:**

1. L
2. W
3. R
4. T
5. I
6. S
7. D
8. T
9. B
10. K
11. C
12. T
13. M
14. A
15. Z
16. A
17. H
18. J

1. G
2. F
3. I
4. B
5. C
6. J
7. E
8. D
9. A
10. H

Chapter Twenty-Eight
The Confident Years
1953–1964

KEY TOPICS

- **Affluent America**
- **The Cold War Goes on: Eisenhower and Kennedy**
- **The Civil Rights Movement**
- **Lyndon Johnson and the Great Society**

CHAPTER NOTES

In the space below, create your own outline of the chapter. Consider the Key Topics above as well as the overall thrust of the chapter and the text's presentation of material.

Multiple Choice: In the blanks below, write the letter of the **best** response.

1. _____ Which of the following was **not** used to describe Dwight Eisenhower's politics?
   a. Progressive Moderation
   b. Compassionate Conservatism
   c. New Republicanism
   d. Dynamic Conservatism

2. _____ In the 1950s, organized labor gained membership because most workers linked their prosperity with participation.
   a. True
   b. False

3. _____ The government's policy regarding Native Americans in the 1950s:
   a. terminated treaties with tribes.
   b. terminated all benefits to most Native Americans except a one-time cash payment.
   c. encouraged migration to large cities.
   d. nurtured growing militancy among many Native Americans.
   e. did all of these things.

4. _____ In the 1950s, Americans accepted the Interstate Highway idea because:
   a. they were tired of poking along two-lane roads and through towns and cities.
   b. they wanted to explore the country with their new cars.
   c. such highways would enable rapid deployment of military vehicles.
   d. such highways would enable rapid evacuation of cities in case of nuclear war.
   e. of all of these reasons.

5. _____ Just as they had during the 1930s, most Americans in the '50s recalled the lessons of the '20s and avoided personal indebtedness.
   a. True
   b. False

6. _____ According to the text, among the artificial, fantasy environments created during the 1950s, one would find:
   a. Las Vegas.
   b. Disneyland.
   c. shopping malls.
   d. nationally franchised food and motel chains.
   e. all of these changes.

7. _____ In the 1950s, American family life:
   a. witnessed a surge in marriage and birth rates.
   b. replaced street corners and taverns with family activities.
   c. centered around the television set.
   d. was seen as a defense against communism.
   e. was all of these.

8. _____ According to the text, the most successful TV format during the 1950s was:
   a. soap operas.
   b. variety shows.
   c. westerns.
   d. situation comedies.
   e. game shows.

9. _____ During the 1950s, American women discovered all of the following **except**:
   a. reliance upon a single bread-winner, and thus a decreased need to work.
   b. increased housework, despite many labor-saving machines.
   c. a decline in their percentage of college degrees and professional jobs.
   d. examples set by popular television role models.
   e. advertising aimed at them.

10. _____ During the 1950s, which of these was **not** considered an effective antidote for communism?
    a. Family life
    b. Prosperity
    c. Sit-ins
    d. Religion
    e. Consumer choices

11. _____ Which of the following often did **not** enjoy the prosperity of the 1950s?
    a. Old people in bug-infested hotels
    b. White families in Appalachia
    c. African Americans in urban ghettos
    d. Hispanic migrant workers
    e. All of these groups

12. _____ The world during the '50s could be described as:
    a. disinterested.
    b. bipolar.
    c. disillusioned.
    d. generally neutral.
    e. bellicose.

13. _____ In his approach to the Cold War, Dwight Eisenhower:
    a. advocated massive (nuclear) retaliation.
    b. wanted to economize on military spending.
    c. relied on superior American technology.
    d. wanted "more bang for the buck."
    e. expressed all of these.

14. _____ "Sputnik" is the Russian word for:
    a. satellite.
    b. vodka.
    c. student.
    d. parliament.
    e. space.

15. _____ Eisenhower continued the diplomacy of Truman in that:
    a. he saw a world caught between two hostile camps.
    b. he accepted existing spheres of communist influence.
    c. he attempted to block communist expansion in the "third world."
    d. he assumed the right and need to intervene in other nations' affairs.
    e. he exhibited all of these notions.

16. _____ Eisenhower refused to intervene in:
    a. Hungary.
    b. Iran.
    c. Quemoy and Matsu.
    d. Guatemala.
    e. Egypt.

17. _____ John F. Kennedy's program of scientific and social progress was called:
   a. the Newer Deal.
   b. the Fair Deal.
   c. the New Frontier.
   d. the Great Society.
   e. a crying shame.

18. _____ Probably the one thing that facilitated Kennedy's election victory over Nixon was:
   a. youth.
   b. experience.
   c. television.
   d. civil rights record.
   e. family values.

19. _____ During the Kennedy years, the Soviets did all of the following **except**:
   a. install missiles on Cuba.
   b. erect the Berlin Wall.
   c. violate an American naval quarantine of Cuba.
   d. put a man in orbit around the earth.
   e. renew nuclear testing.

20. _____ In the case *Brown v. Board of Education*, the Supreme Court:
   a. upheld the 1896 ruling in *Plessy v. Ferguson*.
   b. was narrowly divided in a 5-4 vote.
   c. ruled that separate facilities are inherently unequal.
   d. heard arguments from only white attorneys.
   e. did all of these.

21. _____ Of these post-WWII presidents, the one with the **best** record on civil rights was:
   a. Harry Truman.
   b. Dwight Eisenhower.
   c. John Kennedy.
   d. Lyndon Johnson.
   e. Richard Nixon.

22. _____ Which of these places was **not** the scene of celebrated civil rights milestones?
   a. Little Rock, Arkansas.
   b. Greensboro, North Carolina.
   c. Oklahoma City, Oklahoma.
   d. Montgomery, Alabama.
   e. Selma, Alabama.

23. _____ Birmingham, Alabama, witnessed:
   a. the use of fire hoses and police dogs.
   b. attacks upon "freedom riders."
   c. the arrest of Martin Luther King.
   d. the church bombing that killed four children.
   e. all of these events.

24. _____ In the 1950s, the most lukewarm supporter of desegregation was:
   a. the Presbyterian Church.
   b. the Southern Baptist Convention.
   c. Billy Graham.
   d. John Kennedy.
   e. Lyndon Johnson.

25. ____ According to the text, the assassination of John F. Kennedy was:
    a. unlike any previous presidential murder.
    b. the act of one unbalanced man acting alone.
    c. the product of a conspiracy involving the CIA.
    d. a collusion between the FBI and the Mafia.
    e. carried out by the other guy on the grassy knoll.

26. ____ When he became president, Lyndon Johnson was warmly received by the elites of the Kennedy administration.
    a. True
    b. False

27. ____ As president, Johnson exhibited:
    a. little knowledge of foreign affairs.
    b. more legislative savvy than Kennedy.
    c. ambition and crudeness (and surgical scars).
    d. deep commitment to social equity.
    e. all of these.

28. ____ Johnson's greatest successes as president included all of these **except**:
    a. the Civil Rights Act of 1964.
    b. a landslide reelection in 1964.
    c. the Tonkin Resolution of 1964.
    d. the Voting Rights Act of 1965.
    e. the creation of Medicare and Medicaid.

Chronological Arrangement: Rearrange the list of events below by **rewriting** each item in correct chronological sequence into the blanks provided.

Soviet tanks roll into Hungary   _____

Berlin Wall erected   _____

U-2 spy plane shot down over Russia   _____

Ngo Dinh Diem assassinated   _____

Soviets explode a hydrogen bomb   _____

Gulf of Tonkin incident   _____

Bay of Pigs debacle   _____

Cuban Missile Crisis   _____

Vietnam divided at Geneva   _____

Fidel Castro assumes power in Cuba   _____

Chronological Arrangement: Rearrange the list of events below by **rewriting** each item in correct chronological sequence into the blanks provided.

Woolworth's sit-in starts in Greensboro _____

Medicare/Medicaid created _____

Brown v. Board of Education _____

Civil Rights Act passed _____

Freedom rides begin in the South _____

Interstate Highway system begins _____

Voting Rights Act passed _____

Montgomery bus boycott begins _____

John Kennedy assassinated _____

Integration at Central High School _____

Essay: Read each of the following questions, take some time to organize your thoughts, then compose thorough, meaningful answers for each.

1. In what ways did Urban Renewal help inner cities? In what ways did the changes hurt?

2. How did interstate highways change American cities? American commerce? American life?

3. How did television both reflect and shape American life in the 1950s?

4. Explain the factors that permitted "rock and roll" to become the phenomenon when it did.

5. Explain this statement from the text: "Women wondered how to be both Betty and Marilyn."

6. Why *did* we like Ike? Was his approach to the presidency more like Clinton's or Bush's?

7. How did the U-2 incident illustrate the tendency of the Cold War belligerents to misinterpret each others' actions?

8. Discuss the United States' first steps into Vietnam.

9. Explain how southern states attempted to delay court orders to desegregate.

10. Explain Lyndon Johnson's landslide victory in the election of 1964.

11. Compare and contrast the Cold War views of Dwight Eisenhower and John Kennedy.

12. Compare and contrast the 1950s struggle against polio with that currently against HIV/AIDS.

Matching: Match each item in the left column with the person most likely associated with it.
(Beware: Not all names will be used!)

1. _____ "Dynamic Conservatism"		A.	Barry Goldwater
2. _____ *The Honeymooners*		B.	Billy Graham
3. _____ "Heartbreak Hotel"		C.	George C. Wallace
4. _____ *Rebel Without a Cause*		D.	John Foster Dulles
5. _____ *The Power of Positive Thinking*		E.	Dwight Eisenhower
6. _____ *The Affluent Society*		F.	Betty Friedan
7. _____ "Kitchen Debate"		G.	Jackie Gleason
8. _____ *The Other America*		H.	Michael Harrington
9. _____ *The Feminine Mystique*		I.	Reza Pahlevi
10. _____ "Brinksmanship"		J.	James Dean
11. _____ U-2 (pilot)		K.	John Kenneth Galbraith
12. _____ First human in space		L.	Lee Harvey Oswald
13. _____ *Brown v. Board of Education*		M.	Martin L. King
14. _____ Central High School		N.	Nikita Khrushchev
15. _____ "Standing in the schoolhouse door"		O.	Orval Faubus
16. _____ Montgomery bus boycott		P.	Elvis Presley
17. _____ Shared pulpit with Martin L. King		Q.	"Little Richard"
18. _____ "I Have a Dream"		R.	Rosa Parks
19. _____ Texas School Book Depository		S.	Adlai Stevenson
20. _____ AuH$_2$O		T.	Harry Truman
		U.	Francis Gary Powers
		V.	Norman V. Peale
		W.	Thurgood Marshall
		X.	Xavier Cugat
		Y.	Yuri Gagarin

MULTIPLE CHOICE ANSWERS:

1. B (p. 875)
2. A (pp. 875–876)
3. E (p. 877)
4. E (p. 877)
5. B (p. 877)
6. E (pp. 877–878)
7. E (p. 879)
8. D (p. 879)
9. A (p. 880)
10. C (pp. 879, 881–882)

11. E (p. 882)
12. B (p. 883)
13. E (p. 884)
14. A (p. 885)
15. E (p. 885)
16. A (p. 886)
17. C (p. 889)
18. C (p. 889)
19. C (pp. 890, 892)
20. C (pp. 893–894)

21. D (p. 898)
22. C (pp. 895–896, 900)
23. E (p. 897)
24. D (p. 897)
25. B (p. 898)
26. B (p. 898)
27. E (p. 898)
28. C (pp. 899–900)

CHRONOLOGICAL ARRANGEMENT ANSWERS:

Soviets explode a hydrogen bomb, Vietnam divided at Geneva, Soviet tanks roll into Hungary, Fidel Castro assumes power in Cuba, U-2 spy plane shot down over Russia, Bay of Pigs debacle, Berlin Wall erected, Cuban Missile Crisis, Ngo Dinh Diem assassinated, Gulf of Tonkin incident

CHRONOLOGICAL ARRANGEMENT ANSWERS:

Brown v. Board of Education, Montgomery bus boycott begins, Interstate Highway system begins, Integration at Central High School, Woolworth's sit-in starts in Greensboro, Freedom rides begin in the South, John Kennedy assassinated, Civil Rights Act passed, Medicare/Medicaid created, Voting Rights Act passed

MATCHING ANSWERS:

1. E
2. G
3. P
4. J
5. V
6. K
7. N
8. H
9. F
10. D

11. U
12. Y
13. W
14. O
15. C
16. R
17. B
18. M
19. L
20. A

Chapter Twenty-Nine
Shaken to the Roots
1965–1980

KEY TOPICS

- **The Unraveling of America**
- **1968**
- **Vietnam and Watergate**
- **The Travails of the 1970s**

CHAPTER NOTES

In the space below, create your own outline of the chapter. Consider the Key Topics above as well as the overall thrust of the chapter and the text's presentation of material.

Multiple Choice: In the blanks below, write the letter of the **best** response.

1. _____ Lyndon Johnson pursued military build-up in Vietnam for all these reasons **except**
   a. that Americans were still determined to contain communism.
   b. that he felt obliged to honor Kennedy's commitments.
   c. that he was led to believe that Vietnam could be secured militarily.
   d. that he had no clearly defined domestic agenda.
   e. that he assumed that China was aggressively backing North Vietnam.

2. _____ To win in Vietnam, the American military relied upon
   a. saturation bombing of North Vietnamese targets.
   b. search and destroy tactics.
   c. massive displays of sophisticated firepower.
   d. surveillance, patrols, air strikes, and reinforcements by helicopter.
   e. all of these techniques

3. _____ Opponents of the expanding war did not include any prominent anti-communists or Cold War strategists.
   a. True
   b. False

4. _____ During the Vietnam era, the Selective Service drafted disproportionate numbers of
   a. small-town boys.
   b. working-class boys.
   c. African-American boys.
   d. teenage boys.
   e. all of these groups

5. _____ The group Students for a Democratic Society (SDS)
   a. advocated violent protest from its inception.
   b. shared common ideas with the Black Panthers.
   c. encouraged grassroots action and participatory democracy.
   d. retained its single-issue, anti-war focus.
   e. all of these answers

6. _____ According to the text, many "hippies" were most interested in
   a. rock concerts.
   b. hair.
   c. social reform.
   d. political activism.
   e. drugs.

7. _____ According to the text, youth culture was shaped by
   a. movies.
   b. philosophers.
   c. "mind-expanding" drugs.
   d. music.
   e. all of these forces

8. _____ 1960s communes were most likely to be found in all of these places **except**
   a. the Southwest.
   b. the Pacific Northwest.
   c. upper New England.
   d. the Midwest.

9. _____ According to the text, the sexual revolution of the 1960s eroded the double standard that expected chastity of women but tolerated promiscuity among men.
   a. True
   b. False

10. _____ In 1986, feminists in Atlantic City protested the Miss America pageant by crowning _____ as their "Miss America."
   a. a man
   b. a lesbian
   c. a Holstein
   d. a sheep
   e. Miss Texas

11. _____ The 1969 "Stonewall Rebellion" concerned
   a. Confederate Civil War heroes in Virginia.
   b. journeyman masons and bricklayers in Cleveland.
   c. exotic dancers in New York.
   d. farmers in New England.
   e. patrons of gay bars in New York.

12. _____ The phrase "long, hot summers" concerned
   a. water shortages and rationing.
   b. global warming.
   c. race riots in large cities.
   d. exotic dancers in New York.
   e. threatened strikes in major league baseball.

13. _____ Efforts to be defined through one's own ethnic heritage and not merely as an adjunct of white culture characterized the desires of
   a. African Americans.
   b. Hispanics.
   c. Native Americans.
   d. all of these groups
   e. a and b only

14. _____ From 1969 to 1973, militant Native Americans seized all of the following **except**
   a. Alcatraz Island.
   b. the Bureau of Indian Affairs building.
   c. Mt. Rushmore.
   d. Wounded Knee.

15. _____ In "edge cities" one might find
   a. airports.
   b. hotels and restaurants.
   c. community colleges.
   d. independent school districts.
   e. all of these answers

16. _____ Requiring "one person, one vote," i.e., legislative seats to be apportioned by population, was the ruling by the Supreme court in
   a. *Engel v. Vitale.*
   b. *Baker v. Carr.*
   c. *Abington Township v. Schempp.*
   d. *Marbury v. Madison.*
   e. *Swann v. Charlotte-Mecklenburg Board of Education.*

17. _____ Part of the frustrations of 1968 was a growing awareness among Americans that both the Soviet Union and China were furnishing massive aid to North Vietnam.
    a. True
    b. False

18. _____ Vietnam became the "living room war" because
    a. so many families had sons in the military and thus missing from living rooms.
    b. television brought war realities into American living rooms.
    c. American commanders could use modern technology to direct the war from their own living rooms.
    d. democracy and capitalism required "living room" to expand in southeast Asia.

19. _____ Which of the following was **not** one of the traumas of the traumatic year 1968?
    a. Tet Offensive in Vietnam
    b. assassination of Martin Luther King
    c. assassination of Robert Kennedy
    d. ugly Democratic Convention in Chicago.
    e. killings of Kent State students by the National Guard

20. _____ Which of the following presidents focused on pollution and endangered environments as his primary environmental concern?
    a. John Kennedy
    b. Lyndon Johnson
    c. Richard Nixon
    d. Gerald Ford
    e. Jimmy Carter

21. _____ Upon becoming president in 1969, Richard Nixon immediately began slowly decreasing American military presence in Vietnam.
    a. True
    b. False

22. _____ The foreign policy position of both Richard Nixon and Henry Kissinger could be defined as
    a. pragmatic and realistic.
    b. moral and crusading.
    c. balancing world power.
    d. all of these
    e. a and c only

23. _____ The French word "*détente*," as applied to U.S. foreign policy, means
    a. alliance.
    b. friendship.
    c. easing of tensions.
    d. *Realpolitik.*
    e. stand-off.

24. _____ When a price increase in one key product raises the cost of producing other items, it is called
    a. "demand-pull" inflation.
    b. "cost-push" inflation.
    c. "supply-side" economics.
    d. "voodoo" economics.
    e. a "crying shame."

25. ____ As president, Nixon's main achievement(s) concerned
   a. *détente* with Russia and China.
   b. environmental policies.
   c. revenue-sharing to suburban America.
   d. all of these answers
   e. a and c only

26. ____ Nixon's White House "plumbers"
   a. pursued and harassed Americans on Nixon's "enemies list."
   b. contributed to an atmosphere of lawlessness in the White House.
   c. were only supposed to prevent leaks of information.
   d. cooked up schemes to embarrass political opponents.
   e. all of these answers

27. ____ The specific House impeachment charge(s) against Richard Nixon included
   a. hindering a criminal investigation.
   b. abusing the power of the presidency.
   c. using federal agencies to deprive citizens of their rights.
   d. ignoring congressional subpoenas.
   e. all of these charges

28. ____ Most likely, Gerald Ford's first major act as president was
   a. playing golf.
   b. the Helsinki Accords.
   c. pardoning Nixon.
   d. pardoning draft resisters.
   e. ignoring a recession and high unemployment.

29. ____ Jimmy Carter's main problem(s) as president included
   a. his low-key approach to the office.
   b. his tendency to get mired in details rather than defining broad goals.
   c. his failure to understand the importance of personalities.
   d. his moral intransigence and inability to compromise.
   e. all of these answers

30. ____ Perhaps Carter's greatest triumph as president was
   a. the Camp David Agreement.
   b. the rescue of the Iranian hostages.
   c. SALT II.
   d. the Helsinki Accords.
   e. expanding peanut markets abroad.

31. ____ During the 1970s, more and more Americans established small family farms.
   a. True
   b. False

32. ____ Which of the following presidents was never awarded a Nobel Peace Prize?
   a. Theodore Roosevelt
   b. Woodrow Wilson
   c. John Kennedy
   d. Jimmy Carter

Chronological Arrangement: Re-arrange the list of events below by **re-writing** each item in correct chronological sequence into the blanks provided.

Watts riots in Los Angeles

_____

Democratic Convention in Chicago

_____

John Kennedy assassinated

_____

Watergate break-in

_____

Ronald Reagan elected

_____

Richard Nixon elected

_____

Robert Kennedy assassinated

_____

Gerald Ford pardons Nixon

_____

Martin Luther King assassinated

_____

Jimmy Carter elected president

_____

Chronological Arrangement: Re-arrange the list of events below by **re-writing** each item in correct chronological sequence into the blanks provided.

Tet Offensive

_____

Operation "Rolling Thunder"

_____

Saigon falls to communists

_____

Richard Nixon visits China

_____

Kent State killings

_____

Iran hostage crisis begins

_____

U.S. invades Cambodia

_____

Camp David accords

_____

Arab oil embargo

_____

First moon landing

_____

Essay: Read each of the following questions, take some time to organize your thoughts, then compose thorough, meaningful answers for each.

1. In what ways was the U.S. Vietnam experience similar to that of the British in the American Revolution?

2. Who were some prominent voices of opposition to the war? What were their points?

3. In what way(s) did many youthful members of the 1960s "counterculture" belie their ostensibly revolutionary message?

4. Why did religion — from both western and eastern traditions — appeal to youth in the 1960s?

5. Did 1960s media *reflect* or *shape* popular perceptions of American cities? Or both? Explain.

6. What new directions did the Civil Rights movement take in the mid-1960s?

7. How did the War in Vietnam bring down Lyndon Johnson?

8. Discuss the Democratic Convention in Chicago. Who were the biggest losers politically?

9. Describe the methods employed by Richard Nixon to distract Americans' attention from an unpopular war.

10. Discuss the facets of Nixon's character that led his administration into the Watergate fiasco.

11. Discuss the appeal of Jimmy Carter to Americans weary of scandal and economic hardships.

12. What hard lessons were the United States forced to learn through the period of 1964-1980?

MULTIPLE CHOICE ANSWERS;

1. D (p. 911)	11. E (p. 919)	21. B (p. 927)	31. B (p. 937)
2. E (pp. 912–913)	12. C (p. 920)	22. E (p. 929)	32. C (p. 939)
3. B (p. 914)	13. D (p. 921)	23. C (p. 929)	
4. E (p. 915)	14. C (pp. 922–923)	24. B (p. 930)	
5. C (p. 916)	15. E (p. 923)	25. D (pp. 929–932)	
6. E (p. 917)	16. B (p. 923)	26. E (p. 933)	
7. E (p. 917)	17. B (p. 924)	27. E (p. 934)	
8. D (p. 918)	18. B (p. 924)	28. C (p. 934)	
9. A (p. 919)	19. E (pp. 924, 926)	29. E (p. 936)	
10. D (p. 919)	20. C (p. 931)	30. A (p. 938)	

CHRONOLOGICAL ARRANGEMENT ANSWERS:

John Kennedy assassinated; Watts riots in Los Angeles; Martin Luther King assassinated; Robert Kennedy assassinated; Democratic Convention in Chicago; Richard Nixon elected; Watergate break-in; Gerald Ford pardons Nixon; Jimmy Carter elected president; Ronald Reagan elected

CHRONOLOGICAL ARRANGEMENT ANSWERS:

Operation "Rolling Thunder"; Tet Offensive; First moon landing; U.S. invades Cambodia; Kent State killings; Richard Nixon visits China; Arab oil embargo; Saigon falls to communists; Camp David accords; Iran hostage crisis begins

Chapter Thirty
The Reagan Revolution and a Changing World
1981–1992

KEY TOPICS

- **Reagan's Domestic Agenda**
- **The End of the Cold War**
- **Changing America**
- **Conflicting Values**

CHAPTER NOTES

In the space below, create your own outline of the chapter. Consider the Key Topics above as well as the overall thrust of the chapter and the text's presentation of material.

Multiple Choice: In the blanks below, write the letter of the **best** response.

1. _____ According to the text, American voters voted
   a. *for* Ronald Reagan in 1980.
   b. *against* Jimmy Carter in 1980.
   c. *for* Ronald Reagan in 1984.
   d. *against* Walter Mondale in 1984.
   e. b and c

2. _____ Reagan was able to garner votes from
   a. anti-communist stalwarts from both parties.
   b. those fed up with large, bureaucratic government.
   c. disaffected blue-collar and middle-class voters.
   d. Christian conservatives worried about the nation's directions.
   e. all of these groups

3. _____ In his 1984 book *Losing Ground*, Charles Murray argued that
   a. welfare assistance hurt more than it helped.
   b. welfare encourages government dependency.
   c. welfare discourages individual efforts at self-improvement.
   d. poverty and related problems had actually increased despite massive government programs.
   e. all of these answers

4. _____ To further their message and agenda, Republicans in the 1980s relied upon
   a. radio talk shows and mass mailings.
   b. television news programs.
   c. conservative bias in the media.
   d. door-to-door canvassing.
   e. help from union bosses.

5. _____ Reagan's policy of deregulation affected
   a. the airline industry.
   b. federal lands.
   c. banking.
   d. the environment.
   e. all of these answers

6. _____ Westerners who wanted less government regulation and more opportunities for growth were known as the
   a. Young Guns.
   b. Cheyenne Social Club.
   c. Texas Playboys.
   d. Sagebrush Rebellion.
   e. Watt's on Second.

7. _____ During the 1980s, union membership declined because
   a. owners could play one plant's workers against another's.
   b. owners threatened to move plants to another state or country.
   c. owners could sell out, thus eliminating union contract obligations.
   d. many blue-collar jobs were replaced by machinery.
   e. of all these answers

8. _____ In the 1980s, upwardly-mobile (economically) African Americans often referred to themselves as
   a. an enigma.
   b. yuppies.
   c. buppies.
   d. hippies.
   e. an asterisk.

9. _____ Which was **not** a new musical trend or innovation of the 1980s?
   a. Punk
   b. Grunge
   c. Disco
   d. Hip-hop
   e. Rap

10. _____ During the '80s, the number of homeless Americans increased because
   a. former patients at mental hospitals were released to the streets.
   b. there were new forms of drug abuse.
   c. a boom in downtown real estate left residents of poorer neighborhoods with no other place to go.
   d. many middle-class Americans denied the severity or cause of the problem.
   e. of all of these factors

11. _____ The major domestic agenda of George H. W. Bush became
   a. making conservative appointments to the Supreme Court.
   b. a war on crime and drugs.
   c. a crack-down on illegal immigration.
   d. the enactment of a flat tax rate.
   e. limiting tax increases.

12. _____ During the 1980s, Ronald Reagan's Soviet policy
   a. reflected his Cold War belief that the Soviet Union was a clear and very dangerous threat.
   b. resulted in massive increases in defense spending that the Soviets could not match without going broke.
   c. resulted in stepped-up arming of NATO nations.
   d. resulted in a proposal to create a space-based shield to protect against incoming Soviet missiles.
   e. all of these answers

13. _____ Which of the following was **not** the locus of American intervention in the 1980s?
   a. Kosovo
   b. Nicaragua
   c. Lebanon
   d. Grenada
   e. Panama

14. _____ The new political openness instituted by Mikhail Gorbachev in the Soviet Union was known as
   a. *glasnost*.
   b. *perestroika*.
   c. *sputnik*.
   d. *bolshevism*.

15. ____ Reagan's face-to-face negotiations with Gorbachev eventually culminated in
    a. the first true nuclear disarmament treaty.
    b. the same, continuing mistrust and suspicion that had always characterized the cold war.
    c. the invasion of Grenada.
    d. Russian help in negotiating the release of the Iranian hostages.
    e. boycotting each others' summer Olympic games.

16. ____ By the end of 1989, which of these nations had democratic or non-communist governments?
    a. Czechoslovakia
    b. Romania
    c. Hungary
    d. Poland
    e. all of these nations

17. ____ The final dissolution of the Soviet Union was spurred by
    a. free elections in 1989.
    b. resistance by Boris Yeltsin, president of the Russian Republic.
    c. a failed coup against Mikhail Gorbachev in 1991.
    d. the reunited Germany's decision to join NATO.
    e. the fall of the Berlin Wall.

18. ____ According to the text, the notion that Americans are too impatient to wage a methodical, protracted war may be termed the
    a. "Marshall Plan."
    b. "Reagan Doctrine."
    c. "Vietnam Syndrome."
    d. "Make My Day" law.
    e. "Instant Gratification Syndrome."

19. ____ Which of the following states is usually **not** considered part of the "Sunbelt" that experienced economic and population growth during the 1980s and 1990s?
    a. California
    b. Texas
    c. Florida
    d. Oklahoma
    e. Arizona

20. ____ The term "Silicon Valley" referred to that region of California known for its
    a. military and civilian computer industries.
    b. elective cosmetic surgery industries.
    c. gambling industries.
    d. space exploration industries.
    e. housing materials industries.

21. ____ The Immigration and Nationality Act of 1965 accomplished all of these **except**
    a. abolishing the national quota system.
    b. granting more favorable status to immigrants from western Europe.
    c. giving preference to family reunification.
    d. welcoming immigrants from all nations equally.
    e. welcoming more immigrants from communist countries.

22. ____ During the 1980s, the largest single group of immigrants came from Haiti.
    a. True
    b. False

23. ____ According to the text, American border cities such as El Paso and San Diego suffer financially from their close proximity to their cross-border Mexican neighbors.
   a. True
   b. False

24. ____ According to the text, people in their sixties and seventies who remain sharp, vigorous, and financially secure are called the
   a. "Gray Panthers."
   b. lucky ones.
   c. "young old."
   d. "gen-X-ers."

25. ____ The Equal Rights Amendment failed ratification because
   a. not enough state legislatures voted for it.
   b. of strong opposition by conservative groups.
   c. the time limit expired before enough states could vote for ratification.
   d. all of these reasons
   e. a and b only

26. ____ Which of the following denominations has **not** struggled to maintain membership?
   a. Methodist
   b. Episcopal
   c. Baptist
   d. United Church of Christ
   e. Presbyterian

27. ____ American Catholicism has experienced changes in recent decades because
   a. of the Second Vatican Council.
   b. of the presidency of the popular John Kennedy.
   c. of the increasing presence of Asian and Latino Catholics.
   d. of modernizing trends such as masses in English.
   e. all these factors

28. ____ Which of the following statistics is **not** accurate?
   a. Growing numbers of teenagers became sexually active in the 1970s.
   b. The divorce rate declined after 1980.
   c. Births to teenagers dropped after 1990.
   d. The number of two-parent families declined after 1990.
   e. Most American adults are monogamous.

29. ____ (An) important battleground(s) in the "culture wars" include(s)
   a. "family values."
   b. the role of public schools in shaping societal values.
   c. government funding for "obscene" art.
   d. the recognition and rights of homosexuals.
   e. all of these issues

30. ____ In retrospect, it seems that Americans in the 1980s wanted stability after a decade of unexpected and uncomfortable change.
   a. True
   b. False

Chronological Arrangement: Re-arrange the list of events below by **re-writing** each item in correct chronological sequence into the blanks provided.

Equal Rights Amendment fails

_____

Federal bailout of savings and loans

_____

George H. W. Bush elected

_____

Tax Reform Act passed

_____

Rodney King beaten/L.A. riots

_____

Ronald Reagan becomes president

_____

Reagan survives assassination attempt

_____

Bill Clinton defeats Bush and Perot

_____

Roe v. Wade

_____

Reagan re-elected in landslide

_____

Chronological Arrangement: Re-arrange the list of events below by **re-writing** each item in correct chronological sequence into the blanks provided.

Iran-Contra hearings on TV

_____

Persian Gulf War

_____

Soviet Union dissolves

_____

Iraq invades Kuwait

_____

U.S. invades Grenada

_____

Iranian-held hostages released

_____

U.S. invades Panama

_____

Gorbachev's reforms in the Soviet Union

_____

Berlin Wall dismantled

_____

American hostages captured in Iran

_____

Essay: Read each of the following questions, take some time to organize your thoughts, then compose thorough, meaningful answers for each.

1. Discuss the appeal of Ronald Reagan — as a person, as a candidate, and as president.

2. In general, what do liberals and conservatives believe about business? About the size and proper role of government?

3. Why was the labor movement in "crisis" during the Reagan years?

4. Explain why having a "job for life" became less likely for many Americans during the 1980s.

5. Describe the effects of the Rodney King verdict upon various ethnic groups in Los Angeles.

6. Discuss the reasons for the fall of communism and the Soviet Union in eastern Europe.

7. Discuss the intricate relationship between Ronald Reagan and Mikhail Gorbachev.

8. List and discuss various reasons (obvious and not-so-obvious) for the decision to attack Iraq in 1991.

9. Describe new patterns of immigration to the west coast, the east coast, and the South.

10. Discuss the geographical and economic impact of "the graying of America."

11. Why are there more women in the workforce now than in 1970?

12. Explain the distinctions between "conservative" and "liberal" religious views and expressions.

Matching: Match each description in the left column with the person it most likely describes.
(Beware: Not all names will be used!)

1. ____ "Teflon" president whose name has defined
an economic approach and an era.

2. ____ Vice President (1981-1989); hand-picked success-
sor of #1; failed to win re-election in 1992.

3. ____ Carter's Vice President; "earnest, honest, and dull"
landslide loser of the 1984 presidential election.

4. ____ Congressman who pushed to cut federal economic
regulations to encourage business enterprise.

5. ____ Reagan's controversial Interior Secretary; wanted
less western environmental regulation.

6. ____ Revived the flagging fortunes of the Chrysler Corporation; portrayed the CEO as hero.

7. ____ "Dry-as-dust" Massachusetts governor who lost the
election of 1988 by appearing soft on crime.

8. ____ Marine and NSC staffer who illegally organized aid
for anti-communist "Contras" in Nicaragua.

9. ____ Drug-dealing Panamanian dictator; U.S. troops
ousted him to stand trial in Miami.

10. ____ Charming and chummy Soviet leader; his friendship
with Reagan helped end the Cold War.

11. ____ Russian president who helped put down a 1991
coup attempt against #10 above.

12. ____ Iraq president who seized oil-rich neighboring
Kuwait and threatened other Arab neighbors.

13. ____ Conservative television evangelist who sought
the Republican nomination in 1988.

14. ____ Liberal Chicago minister and civil rights leader
who sought the Democratic nomination in 1988.

15. ____ Virginia pastor, founder of the Moral Majority; his
open letter represents conservative values.

A. Al Sharpton

B. George Bush

C. Jimmy Carter

D. Michael Dukakis

E. Earl Butts

F. Jerry Falwell

G. Mikhail Gorbachev

H. Saddam Hussein

I. Lee Iacocca

J. Jesse Jackson

K. Jack Kemp

L. Melvin Laird

M. Walter Mondale

N. Manuel Noriega

O. Oliver North

P. Pat Robertson

Q. Elizabeth II

R. Ronald Reagan

S. David Stockman

T. "The Donald" (Trump)

U. Uday Hussein

V. Ivan Boesky

W. James Watt

X. Richard Nixon

Y. Boris Yeltsin

MULTIPLE CHOICE ANSWERS:

1. E (p. 948)	11. B (p. 957)	21. B (p. 968)
2. E (p. 949)	12. E (pp. 958–960)	22. B (p. 968)
3. E (p. 950)	13. A (pp. 960–961)	23. B (p. 970)
4. A (p. 951)	14. A (p. 961)	24. C (p. 970)
5. E (p. 951)	15. A (p. 962)	25. D (p. 971)
6. D (p. 951)	16. A (p. 963)	26. C (p. 973)
7. E (pp. 952–953)	17. C (p. 963)	27. E (p. 973)
8. C (p. 954)	18. C (p. 966)	28. D (p. 976)
9. C (p. 954)	19. D (pp. 966–967)	29. E (p. 976)
10. E (p. 956)	20. A (p. 968)	30. A (p. 976)

CHRONOLOGICAL ARRANGEMENT ANSWERS:

Roe v. Wade; Ronald Reagan becomes president; Reagan survives assassination attempt; Equal Rights Amendment fails; Reagan re-elected in landslide; Tax Reform Act passed; George H. W. Bush elected; Federal bailout of savings and loans; Rodney King beaten/L.A. riots; Bill Clinton defeats Bush and Perot

CHRONOLOGICAL ARRANGEMENT ANSWERS:

American hostages captured in Iran; Iranian-held hostages released; U.S. invades Grenada; Gorbachev's reforms in the Soviet Union; Iran-Contra hearings on TV; Berlin Wall dismantled; U.S. invades Panama;, Iraq invades Kuwait;, Persian Gulf War; Soviet Union dissolves

MATCHING ANSWERS:

1. R
2. B
3. M
4. K
5. W
6. I
7. D
8. O
9. N
10. G
11. Y
12. H
13. P
14. J
15. F

Chapter Thirty-One
Complacency and Crisis
1993–2005

KEY TOPICS

- Politics: Left and Right of Center (Slightly)
- The Economy in the 1990s
- New Millennium/New President
- The Post-"9/11" World

CHAPTER NOTES

In the space below, create your own outline of the chapter. Consider the Key Topics above as well as the overall thrust of the chapter and the text's presentation of material.

Multiple Choice: In the blanks below, write the letter of the **best** response.

1. _____ In American presidential politics, it has proven to be axiomatic that
   a. a candidate should portray himself as a centrist.
   b. a candidate should try to avoid being seen as an extremist.
   c. voters vote "from the pocketbook."
   d. voters can switch back and forth between the major parties.
   e. all of these answers

2. _____ Which presidential election of the 1990s represented the triumph of the "baby boom" generation over the World War II generation?
   a. 1992
   b. 1996
   c. both elections
   d. neither election

3. _____ Which election did Bill Clinton win by more than 50% of the popular vote?
   a. 1992
   b. 1996
   c. both elections
   d. neither election

4. _____ Where were U.S. troops **not** deployed during the 1990s?
   a. Rwanda
   b. Somalia
   c. Kuwait
   d. Bosnia
   e. Kosovo

5. _____ Which of the following Clinton initiatives was **not** enacted?
   a. The Family and Medical Leave Act
   b. expanded Earned Income Tax Credit
   c. college student aid program
   d. comprehensive national health care plan
   e. domestic Peace Corps

6. _____ During the 1990s, the biggest contributor to America's rising prison population was
   a. domestic terrorism.
   b. gun control violations.
   c. the war on illegal drugs.
   d. drive-by shootings.
   e. the Clinton administration.

7. _____ Special Prosecutor Kenneth Starr investigated the Clintons' involvement in
   a. an Arkansas land development scheme.
   b. the firing of the White House travel office staff.
   c. the suicide of a White House staffer.
   d. the president's womanizing.
   e. all of these matters

8. _____ According to the text, a majority of Americans disapproved of Bill Clinton's conduct of his personal life but did not think his activities justified removal from office.
   a. True
   b. False

317

9. ____ The turn-of-the-century fear that the global computer network was vulnerable to collapse was known as
   a. "Y2K."
   b. "the millennium bug."
   c. the "M&M" crisis.
   d. all of these answers
   e. a and b

10. ____ During the 1990s, the gap between rich and poor Americans narrowed slightly.
    a. True
    b. False

11. ____ Which of the following is **not** considered a "service sector" job?
    a. teaching
    b. fast-food workers
    c. advertising
    d. farmers
    e. child-care workers

12. ____ Which of the following is **not** considered a "high-tech" occupation?
    a. chemical engineering
    b. bioengineering and genetic engineering
    c. aeronautics and space exploration
    d. farming
    e. pharmaceuticals

13. ____ Which of the following industries is considered the epitome of the "sunrise" economy?
    a. petroleum
    b. automobiles
    c. electronics
    d. farming
    e. clothing

14. ____ In which administration was the greatest percentage of women and minorities represented?
    a. Ronald Reagan's
    b. George Bush's
    c. Bill Clinton's
    d. George W. Bush's

15. ____ About how many Americans are there right now?
    a. 180 million
    b. 200 million
    c. 290 million
    d. 310 million
    e. 500 million

16. ____ Which of the following is **not** one of the fastest growing states in population?
    a. Nevada
    b. Arizona
    c. Colorado
    d. Utah
    e. Montana

17. _____ Which is(are) the region(s) with the slowest population growth?
    a. the West
    b. Appalachia
    c. the Great Plains
    d. the Southeast
    e. b and c

18. _____ The fastest-growing group in population is
    a. Hispanics.
    b. Asians.
    c. African Americans.
    d. eastern Europeans.
    e. Native Americans.

19. _____ The nomination of Clarence Thomas to the Supreme Court was controversial
    because
    a. he is black.
    b. his legal background was undistinguished.
    c. Senate Democrats could not tolerate his conservative positions on key issues.
    d. he had allegedly harassed a female co-worker sexually.
    e. c and d

20. _____ Which of the following African Americans was not the mayor of a large city?
    a. Carl Stokes
    b. Jesse Jackson
    c. Tom Bradley
    d. Maynard Jackson
    e. Coleman Young

21. _____ In 1994, California's controversial "Proposition 187" cut off state funding for
    a. education and health care for illegal immigrants.
    b. bilingual education.
    c. reparations payments for past racial injustices.
    d. subsidies for private utilities companies.
    e. "performance-enhancing" steroids in professional sports.

22. _____ Often, members of minority groups oppose affirmative action because
    a. it undermines the legitimacy of their successes.
    b. it suggests they receive jobs or contracts because of race rather than by merit.
    c. they do not consider diversity to be a legitimate objective.
    d. they prefer to conduct business within their own circles.
    e. a and b

23. _____ According to the text, the United States entered the twenty-first century
    a. divided.
    b. balanced.
    c. with extremes of opinion.
    d. with a core of basic goals and values.
    e. all of these answers

24. _____ According to the text, in the election of 2000, both candidates
    a. differed in details rather than broad goals.
    b. targeted their campaigns at middle Americans.
    c. offered to cut taxes as well as the size of government.
    d. promised to protect Social Security.
    e. all of these answers

25. _____ The fiscal policies of George W. Bush were like those of Ronald Reagan, in that they featured
   a. "supply-side" stimuli.
   b. moves to deregulate the economy.
   c. tax cuts for most Americans.
   d. all of these answers
   e. a and b only

26. _____ In foreign policy, Bush demonstrated a "go-it-alone" philosophy by
   a. reducing restrictions on U.S. business and its military.
   b. claiming the right to act militarily to preempt potential threats.
   c. withdrawing from the Kyoto environmental agreement.
   d. reviving Reagan's "SDI" concept.
   e. all of these answers

27. _____ According to the authors of the text, regarding the attacks of September 11, 2001
   a. it is difficult to separate legitimate "signals" from the usual flood of intelligence.
   b. it is easier to read warnings after an event has occurred.
   c. the attacks were just as unpredictable as the Pearl Harbor attack in 1941.
   d. all of these answers
   e. a and b only

28. _____ After the September 11th attacks, President Bush seemed to blame the catastrophe on all Muslims everywhere.
   a. True
   b. False

29. _____ Which of the following was **not** named by Bush as part of the axis of evil?
   a. Iraq
   b. Iran
   c. Afghanistan
   d. North Korea

30. _____ Bush's victory in the election of 2004 was more solid than that of 2000.
   a. True
   b. False

31. _____ The axiom "It is possible to win the war (militarily) but lose the peace" may be validated by
   a. the American Civil War.
   b. World War One.
   c. the Vietnam War.
   d. the war in Iraq.
   e. all of these answers

32. _____ In asserting the United States' duty to extend democracy throughout the world, George W. Bush may have been echoing the thoughts of
   a. Woodrow Wilson.
   b. Franklin Roosevelt.
   c. John Kennedy.
   d. Jimmy Carter.
   e. all of these predecessors

Chronological Arrangement: Re-arrange the list of events below by **re-writing** each item in correct chronological sequence into the blanks provided.

U.S.-led Coalition invades Iraq   _____

"9/11"   _____

George Bush defeats Al Gore   _____

House impeaches Bill Clinton   _____

Bill Clinton defeats Bob Dole   _____

Republicans' "Contract with America"   _____

U.S. joins NAFTA   _____

Bill Clinton defeats George Bush   _____

World Wide Web begins   _____

First CNN broadcast   _____

Essay: Read each of the following questions, take some time to organize your thoughts, then compose thorough, meaningful answers for each.

1. Explain why American voters tend to reject "extremist" candidates in favor of centrists.

2. Why do Americans like having the President from one party and the Congress from the other?

3. Describe the Republican Congress' "Contract With America." How did Democratic opponents manage to paint these initiatives as "extremism"?

4. Argue *both sides* of the debate over the death penalty.

5. In your opinion, what was responsible for the prosperity of the 1990s? Was it "Clintonomics," or "Reaganomics"?

6. In what ways do Americans demonstrate that theirs is an "instant society"?

7. Argue *for and against* "free trade."

8. In what ways does "grassroots politics" encourage participation by women?

9. Opinion: Should government be in the business of guaranteeing *equality of opportunity*, or *equality of outcome*? Or both?

10. Argue *both sides* of the affirmative action debate.

11. Argue *both sides* of the debate over school vouchers.

12. In what ways is the Middle East difficulty linked to U.S. support of Israel?

13. Opinion: Is it possible to write recent history objectively? Explain your position with examples.

Matching: Match each description in the left column with the person it most likely describes. (Beware: Not all names will be used!)

1. _____ Reagan's vice president; last politician of the World War II generation to win the White House.

2. _____ Texas billionaire whose independent campaign in 1992 was on-again-off-again.

3. _____ Won the first of two presidential terms in 1992 by emphasizing voters' economic health.

4. _____ Former (now deceased) Yugoslav president, tried for "ethnic cleansing" war crimes in Kosovo.

5. _____ Her controversial national health care plan contained "something for everyone to dislike."

6. _____ Georgia House Speaker whose "Contract With America" led to a Republican Congress in 1994.

7. _____ Another World War II era senator from Kansas; his loss in the election of 1996 was a replay of 1992.

8. _____ Probably as revenge for a government action in Waco, he bombed a federal building in Oklahoma.

9. _____ White House intern whose affair with the president led to accusations of perjury, obstruction of justice.

10. _____ As governor of Texas, this presidential son allowed a record number of executions.

11. _____ Arizona judge appointed by Reagan as the first female member of the Supreme Court.

12. _____ New York Congresswoman; the first female to appear as a candidate on a major party ticket.

13. _____ Former vice president who lost the 2000 election in a controversial Florida recount and re-recount.

14. _____ Saudi businessman whose hatred of the United States led to the mass murders of "9/11."

15. _____ 43rd President; drove Saddam Hussein from power in Iraq; defeated John Kerry for a second term.

A. Monica Lewinsky

B. Sandra Day O'Connor

C. Timothy McVeigh

D. Donna Rice

E. Geraldine Ferraro

F. Al Gore

G. Gennifer Flowers

H. George H. W. Bush

I. Ross Perot

J. Paula Jones

K. Kathleen Willey

L. Jessica Hahn

M. Marilyn Monroe

N. George W. Bush

O. Hillary Rodham Clinton

P. Peggy O'Neil

Q. Walter Jenkins

R. Newt Gingrich

S. Bill Clinton

T. Slobodan Milosevic

U. Osama bin Laden

V. Maria Halpin

W. Charlotte Corday

X. Christine Keeler

Y. Bob Dole

Z. Rachel Jackson

MULTIPLE CHOICE ANSWERS:

1. E (p. 983)
2. C (pp. 984, 987)
3. D (pp. 984, 987)
4. A (p. 985)
5. D (p. 986)
6. C (p. 988)
7. E (p. 989)
8. A (pp. 989–990)
9. E (p. 990)
10. A (p. 991)
11. D (p. 991)
12. D (p. 993)
13. C (p. 992)
14. D (pp. 997, 1000)
15. C (p. 998)
16. E (p. 998)
17. E (p. 998)
18. A (p. 998)
19. E (p. 999)
20. B (pp. 1000–1001)
21. A (p. 1003)
22. E (p. 1004)
23. E (p. 1004)
24. E (p. 1005)
25. D (pp. 1005–1006)
26. E (p. 1006)
27. D (p. 1007)
28. B (p. 1008)
29. C (p. 1009)
30. A (p. 1010)
31. E (p. 1009)
32. E (p. 1013)

CHRONOLOGICAL ARRANGEMENT ANSWERS:

First CNN broadcast
World Wide Web begins
Bill Clinton defeats George Bush
U.S. joins NAFTA
Republicans' "Contract with America"
Bill Clinton defeats Bob Dole
House impeaches Bill Clinton
George Bush defeats Al Gore
"9/11"
U.S.-led Coalition invades Iraq

MATCHING ANSWERS:

1. H
2. I
3. S
4. T
5. O
6. R
7. Y
8. C
9. A
10. N
11. B
12. E
13. F
14. U
15. N